110 Prostate Cancer Juice and Salad Recipes:

The Cancer-Fighting Guide to a Better Life

By

Joe Correa CSN

COPYRIGHT

© 2019 Live Stronger Faster Inc.

All rights reserved

Reproduction or translation of any part of this work beyond that permitted by section 107 or 108 of the 1976 United States Copyright Act without the permission of the copyright owner is unlawful.

This publication is designed to provide accurate and authoritative information in regard to the subject matter covered. It is sold with the understanding that neither the author nor the publisher is engaged in rendering medical advice. If medical advice or assistance is needed, consult with a doctor. This book is considered a guide and should not be used in any way detrimental to your health. Consult with a physician before starting this nutritional plan to make sure it's right for you.

ACKNOWLEDGEMENTS

This book is dedicated to my friends and family that have had mild or serious illnesses so that you may find a solution and make the necessary changes in your life.

110 Prostate Cancer Juice and Salad Recipes:

The Cancer-Fighting Guide to a Better Life

By

Joe Correa CSN

CONTENTS

Copyright

Acknowledgements

About The Author

Introduction

Commitment

110 Prostate Cancer Juice and Salad Recipes: The Cancer-Fighting Guide to a Better Life

Additional Titles from This Author

ABOUT THE AUTHOR

After years of Research, I honestly believe in the positive effects that proper nutrition can have over the body and mind. My knowledge and experience has helped me live healthier throughout the years and which I have shared with family and friends. The more you know about eating and drinking healthier, the sooner you will want to change your life and eating habits.

Nutrition is a key part in the process of being healthy and living longer so get started today. The first step is the most important and the most significant.

INTRODUCTION

110 Prostate Cancer Juice and Salad Recipes: The Cancer-Fighting Guide to a Better Life

By Joe Correa CSN

Cancer, in general, is a well-known disease that attacks many organs and other parts of our body, somehow it increases the abnormal growth of cells causing the spread of carcinoma in a process called metastases; although there are many treatments for cancer they are extremely invasive, and can many times kill good cells in the process.

This extremely serious disease is the third leading cause of cancer death in the US. These statistics suggest that taking care of your reproductive health and recognizing the symptoms of prostate problems is vital for preventing these complications.

The most common symptoms of prostate problems and cancer include urination abnormalities, pain, painful ejaculation, pelvic or abdominal pain, erectile dysfunction, extremity swelling, and blood in urine or semen. Although not all of these symptoms indicate prostate cancer, they might be a sign of some serious medical conditions that require an immediate medical intervention. Prostate cancer can only be diagnosed by tissue biopsy.

The question is what can you do to prevent prostate cancer? The answer lies in a proper diet. Our body is a truly fantastic organism that has the ability to defend and cure itself. This is why it's crucial to help your immune system to get stronger and boost your overall health.

Eating the right amounts of fruits and vegetables will definitely reduce the risk of prostate cancer. The recommended daily amount of fresh fruits and vegetables is about 4-5 cups. Green, red and orange fruits and vegetables are loaded with carotenoids which are especially beneficial for prostate cancer. Some of the best juice ingredients include: spinach, kale, dandelion greens, oranges, grapefruits, berries, carrots, and tomatoes. Most of these ingredients have a relatively neutral taste and can easily be combined with different herbs and spices for a superb taste.

You will find that these juice and salad recipes will provide you with the necessary nutrients to enjoy a healthier and more vital life. Enjoy these recipes and share them with the ones you love!

COMMITMENT

In order to improve my condition, I *(your name)*, commit to eating more of these foods on a daily basis and to exercise at least 30 minutes daily:

- Berries (especially blueberries), peaches, cherries, apples, apricots, oranges, lemon juice, grapefruit, tangerines, mandarins, pears, etc.
- Broccoli, spinach, collard greens, sweet potatoes, avocado, artichoke, baby corn, carrots, celery, cauliflower, onions, etc.
- Whole grains, steel-cut oats, oatmeal, quinoa, barley, etc.
- Black beans, red bean beans, garbanzo beans, lentils, etc.
- Nuts and seeds including: walnuts, cashews, flaxseeds, sesame seeds, etc.
- Fish
- 8 – 10 glasses of water

Sign here

X_____

110 PROSTATE CANCER JUICE AND SALAD RECIPES: THE CANCER-FIGHTING GUIDE TO A BETTER LIFE

JUICE RECIPES

1. **Tomato Beet Juice**

Ingredients:

4 cherry tomatoes, halved

2 whole beets, sliced

1 cup of watercress, torn

1 rosemary sprig

1 oz of water

Preparation:

Wash the tomatoes and remove the stems. Cut each in half and set aside.

Wash and trim off the beets. Cut the green parts and cut into thin slices. Set aside.

Place the watercress in a colander and wash under cold water. Torn with hands and set aside.

Now, combine tomatoes, beets, watercress, and rosemary in a juicer. Process until well juiced. Transfer to a serving glass and stir in the water. You can add some salt if you like, but it's optional.

Refrigerate for 10 minutes before serving.

Nutritional information per serving: Kcal: 63, Protein: 4.1g, Carbs: 18.7g, Fats: 0.4g

2.   Carrot Celery Juice

Ingredients:

1 large carrot, sliced

1 large celery, chopped

1 cup of fresh kale, chopped

1 small Granny Smith's apple, cored

1 tbsp of liquid honey

Preparation:

Wash and peel the carrot. Cut into thin slices and set aside.

Wash the celery and cut into bite-sized pieces. Set aside.

Rinse the kale under cold running water using a colander. Slightly drain and torn with hands. Set aside.

Wash the apple and cut lengthwise in half. Remove the core and cut into bite-sized pieces. Set aside.

Now, combine carrot, celery, kale, and apple in a juicer and process until juiced. Transfer to a serving glass and stir in the honey.

Add some ice and serve immediately.

Nutritional information per serving: Kcal: 179, Protein: 4.6g, Carbs: 34.3g, Fats: 1.1g

3. Asparagus Grapefruit Juice

Ingredients:

1 cup of asparagus, trimmed and chopped

1 whole grapefruit, peeled

1 whole lime, peeled

1 whole leek, chopped

1 oz of water

Preparation:

Wash the asparagus and trim off the woody ends. Chop into small pieces and set aside.

Peel the grapefruit and divide into wedges. Cut each wedge in half and set aside.

Peel the lime and cut lengthwise in half. Set aside.

Wash the leek and cut into bite-sized pieces. Set aside.

Now, combine asparagus, grapefruit, lime, and leek in a juicer and process until well juiced. Transfer to a serving glass and stir in the water.

Add some honey if you like, but it's optional.

Refrigerate for 10 minutes before serving.

Enjoy!

Nutritional information per serving: Kcal: 161, Protein: 6.3g, Carbs: 47.7g, Fats: 0.8g

4. Dandelion Juice

Ingredients:

1 cup of fresh dandelion greens, torn

2 medium-sized celery stalks, chopped

1 whole lemon, peeled

1 small Granny Smith's apple, cored

1 cup of cucumber, sliced

Preparation:

Wash dandelion greens thoroughly and torn with hands into small pieces. Set aside.

Wash the celery and cut into bite-sized pieces. Set aside.

Peel the lemon and cut lengthwise in half. Set aside.

Wash the apple and cut in half. Remove the core and cut into bite-sized pieces. Set aside.

Wash the cucumber and cut into thin slices. Fill the measuring cup and reserve the rest for later.

Now, combine dandelions, celery, lemon, apple, and cucumber in a juicer and process until juiced.

Transfer to a serving glass and add some crushed ice before serving.

Nutritional information per serving: Kcal: 97, Protein: 2.9g, Carbs: 29.7g, Fats: 0.7g

5. Broccoli Banana Juice

Ingredients:

1 cup of broccoli, chopped

1 large banana, sliced

1 small green apple, cored

1 small ginger knob, peeled

1 tbsp of liquid honey

Preparation:

Wash the broccoli and trim off the outer layers. Cut into small pieces and fill the measuring cup. Reserve the rest for later.

Peel the banana and cut into small slices. Set aside.

Wash the apple and cut in half. Remove the core and cut into bite-sized pieces. Set aside.

Peel the ginger knob and set aside.

Now, combine broccoli, banana, apple, and ginger in a juicer and process until well juiced. Transfer to a serving glass and stir in the honey.

Refrigerate for 10 minutes before serving.

Nutritional information per serving: Kcal: 261, Protein: 4.8g, Carbs: 57.7g, Fats: 1.1g

6. Green Tea Juice

Ingredients:

1 tsp of green tea

2 tbsp of hot water

2 whole kiwis, peeled

1 medium-sized pear, chopped

1 cup of fresh spinach, torn

1 cup of fresh mint, roughly chopped

1 whole lime, peeled

Preparation:

Combine green tea and hot water in a small bowl. Stir well and set aside to soak for 3 minutes.

Peel the kiwis and cut lengthwise in half. Set aside.

Wash the pear and remove the core. Cut into bite-sized pieces and set aside.

Wash the spinach under cold running water using a colander. Torn with hands and set aside.

Wash the mint and roughly chop it. Fill the measuring cup

and reserve the rest for later.

Peel the lime and cut lengthwise in half. Set aside.

Now, combine green tea mixture, kiwis, pear, spinach, mint, and lime in a juicer and process until juiced. Transfer to a serving glass and add some ice before serving.

Enjoy!

Nutritional information per serving: Kcal: 195, Protein: 9.4g, Carbs: 62.4g, Fats: 2.1g

7. Pomegranate Asparagus Juice

Ingredients:

1 cup of pomegranate seeds

1 cup of fresh asparagus, trimmed and chopped

1 whole lemon, peeled

1 tbsp of liquid honey

1 oz of water

Preparation:

Cut the top of the pomegranate fruit using a sharp paring knife. Slice down to each of the white membranes inside of the fruit. Pop the seeds into a measuring cup and set aside.

Wash the asparagus and trim off the woody ends. Cut into bite-sized pieces and set aside.

Peel the lemon and cut into quarters. Set aside.

Now, combine pomegranate seeds, asparagus, and lemon in a juicer and process until well juiced. Transfer to a serving glass and stir in the honey and water.

Add some ice and enjoy!

Nutritional information per serving: Kcal: 145, Protein: 5.1g, Carbs: 26.8g, Fats: 1.3g

8. Spinach Tomato Juice

Ingredients:

1 cup of fresh spinach, chopped

6 cherry tomatoes, halved

1 cup of cucumber, sliced

1 small ginger knob, peeled

¼ tsp of salt

Preparation:

Wash the spinach thoroughly under cold running water. Slightly drain and chop into small pieces. Set aside.

Wash the cherry tomatoes and remove the stems. Cut each tomato in half and set aside.

Wash the cucumber and cut into thin slices. Fill the measuring cup and reserve the rest for later.

Now, combine spinach, tomatoes, cucumber, and ginger in a juicer and process until juiced. Transfer to a serving glass and stir in the salt.

Serve immediately.

Nutritional information per serving: Kcal: 52, Protein: 7.4g, Carbs: 14.5g, Fats: 1.1g

9. Watermelon Blueberry Juice

Ingredients:

1 cup of watermelon, cubed

2 cups of blueberries

1 whole lime, peeled

1 cup of fresh basil, torn

¼ tsp of cayenne pepper, ground

1 oz of water

Preparation:

Cut one large watermelon wedge. Using a sharp paring knife, peel and cut into small cubes. Remove the seeds and set aside. Place the blueberries in a large colander. Rinse well under cold running water and set aside. Peel the lime and cut lengthwise in half. Set aside. Wash the basil and roughly torn it with hands. Set aside.

Now, combine watermelon, blueberries, lime, and basil in a juicer. Process until juiced. Transfer to a serving glass and stir in the cayenne pepper and water.

Refrigerate for 10 minutes before serving.

Nutritional information per serving: Kcal: 198, Protein: 4.1g, Carbs: 58.7g, Fats: 1.4g

10. Carrot Plum Juice

Ingredients:

1 cup of baby carrots, sliced

4 whole plum, chopped

1 cup of Romaine lettuce, shredded

1 cup of mustard greens, torn

1 oz of water

Preparation:

Wash and peel the carrots. Cut into thin slices and fill the measuring cup. Reserve the rest in the refrigerator.

Wash the plums and cut each in half. Remove the pits and set aside.

Combine lettuce and mustard greens in a large colander. Rinse well under cold running water. Shred the lettuce torn the mustard greens using hands. Set aside.

Now, combine carrots, plums, lettuce, and mustard greens in a juicer and process until juiced. Transfer to a serving glass and stir in the water.

Serve cold.

Nutritional information per serving: Kcal: 128, Protein: 4.8g, Carbs: 39.1g, Fats: 1.3g

11. Pepper Avocado Juice

Ingredients:

2 medium-sized red bell peppers, chopped

1 cup of avocado, sliced

1 cup of purple cabbage, chopped

1 whole leek, chopped

1 whole lime, peeled

Preparation:

Wash the peppers and cut in half. Remove the seeds and cut into small pieces. Set aside.

Peel the avocado and cut lengthwise in half. Cut into thin slices and reserve the rest in the refrigerator. Set aside.

Wash the cabbage thoroughly and chop into small pieces. Set aside.

Wash the leek and cut into bite-sized pieces. Set aside.

Peel the lime and cut lengthwise in half. Set aside.

Now, combine peppers, avocado, cabbage, leek, and lime in a juicer and process until juiced. Transfer to a serving glass and refrigerate for 15 minutes before serving.

Enjoy!

Nutritional information per serving: Kcal: 327, Protein: 8.1g, Carbs: 49.6g, Fats: 22.5g

12. Grapefruit Mango Juice

Ingredients:

1 whole grapefruit, peeled

1 cup of mango, cut into chunks

1 cup of fresh mint, roughly chopped

1 large banana, peeled

2 large strawberries, chopped

Preparation:

Peel the grapefruit and divide into wedges. Cut each wedge in half and set aside.

Peel the mango and cut into small chunks. Fill the measuring cup and reserve the rest in the refrigerator. Set aside.

Wash the mint roughly and torn with hands. Set aside.

Peel the banana and cut into small pieces. Set aside.

Wash the strawberries and remove the stems. Cut into bite-sized pieces and set aside.

Now, combine grapefruit, mango, mint, banana, and strawberries in a juicer and process until juiced. Transfer to a serving glass and add some ice cubes before serving.

Enjoy!

Nutritional information per serving: Kcal: 301, Protein: 5.9g, Carbs: 88.5g, Fats: 1.7g

13. Beet Lemon Juice

Ingredients:

1 whole beet, sliced

1 whole lemon, peeled

1 cup of cucumber, sliced

1 medium-sized orange, peeled

1 tbsp of liquid honey

Preparation:

Wash the beet and trim off the green parts. Cut into thin slices and set aside.

Peel the lemon and cut into quarters. Set aside.

Wash the cucumber and cut into thin slices. Fill the measuring cup and reserve the rest in the refrigerator.

Peel the orange and divide into wedges. Cut each wedge in half and set aside.

Now, combine beet, lemon, cucumber, and orange in a juicer and process until juiced. Transfer to a serving glass and stir in the honey.

Add some ice and serve immediately.

Nutritional information per serving: Kcal: 154, Protein: 3.5g, Carbs: 30.5g, Fats: 0.5g

14. Green Bean Juice

Ingredients:

1 cup of green beans, chopped

1 medium-sized Granny Smith's apple, cored

1 medium-sized celery stalk, cut into bite-sized pieces

1 cup of fresh spinach, chopped

Preparation:

Wash the green beans and chop into bite-sized pieces. Fill the measuring cup and reserve the rest for later.

Wash the apple and cut in half. Remove the core and cut into small chunks. Set aside.

Wash the celery and cut into bite-sized pieces. Set aside.

Wash the spinach thoroughly under cold running water. Chop into small pieces and fill the measuring cup. Reserve the rest for later.

Now, combine green beans, apple, celery, and spinach in a juicer and process until well juiced. Transfer to serving glass and add some ice before serving.

Enjoy!

Nutritional information per serving: Kcal: 140, Protein: 8.5g, Carbs: 37.3g, Fats: 1.4g

15. Pepper Kale Juice

Ingredients:

1 medium-sized red bell pepper, chopped

1 cup of fresh kale, chopped

1 cup of parsley, torn

1 large celery stalk, chopped

1 cup of cucumber, sliced

1 oz of water

Preparation:

Wash the bell pepper and cut lengthwise in half. Scrape out the seeds and remove the stem. Cut into bite-sized pieces and set aside.

Wash the kale thoroughly under cold running water. Slightly drain and chop it into small pieces. Set aside.

Wash the parsley and torn with hands. Fill the measuring cup and reserve the rest for later.

Wash the celery stalk and chop it into bite-sized pieces. Set aside.

Wash the cucumber and cut into thin slices. Fill the

measuring cup and reserve the rest for later.

Now, combine bell pepper, kale, parsley, celery, and cucumber in a juicer and process until juiced. Transfer to a serving glass and stir in the water. Add some ice and serve immediately.

Enjoy!

Nutritional information per serving: Kcal: 77, Protein: 6.6g, Carbs: 20.6g, Fats: 1.6g

16. Basil Zucchini Juice

Ingredients:

1 cup of fresh basil, chopped

1 medium-sized zucchini, sliced

1 whole lemon, peeled

1 whole lime, peeled

1 oz of water

Preparation:

Wash the basil thoroughly under cold running water. Slightly drain and chop into small pieces. Set aside.

Wash the zucchini and cut into thin slices. Set aside.

Peel the lemon and lime. Cut each fruit into quarters and set aside.

Now, combine basil, zucchini, lemon, and lime in a juicer. Process until well juiced. Transfer to a serving glass and stir in the water.

Refrigerate for 10 minutes before serving.

Nutritional information per serving: Kcal: 50, Protein: 3.9g, Carbs: 15.8g, Fats: 0.9g

17. Blueberry Grape Juice

Ingredients:

1 cup of blueberries

1 cup of black grapes

1 small Golden Delicious apple, cored

¼ tsp of cinnamon, ground

Preparation:

Wash the blueberries using a colander. Slightly drain and set aside.

Wash the grapes and fill the measuring cup. Reserve the rest for later.

Wash the apple and cut in half. Remove the core and cut into bite-sized pieces. Set aside.

Now, combine blueberries, grapes, and apple in a juicer and process until juiced. Transfer to a serving glass and stir in the cinnamon.

Add some ice before serving and enjoy!

Nutritional information per serving: Kcal: 191, Protein: 2.1g, Carbs: 54.7g, Fats: 1g

18. Mango Raspberry Juice

Ingredients:

1 cup of mango, chunked

1 cup of raspberries

1 small peach, pitted

3 whole apricots, chopped

Preparation:

Peel the mango and cut into small chunks. Fill the measuring cup and reserve the rest for later.

Wash the raspberries using a colander. Slightly drain and fill the measuring cup. Reserve the rest in the refrigerator or freezer for later.

Wash the peach and cut in half. Remove the pit and cut into bite-sized pieces. Set aside.

Wash the apricots and cut in half. Remove the pits and cut in quarters. Set aside.

Now, combine mango, raspberries, peach, and apricots in a juicer and process until juiced. Transfer to a serving glass refrigerate for 10 minutes before serving.

You can garnish with some fresh mint if you like, but it's optional.

Nutritional information per serving: Kcal: 206, Protein: 5.5g, Carbs: 63.5g, Fats: 2.1g

19.   Pineapple Beet Juice

Ingredients:

1 cup of pineapple, chunked

1 whole beet, sliced

1 small orange, wedged

2 tbsp of coconut water

¼ tsp of ginger, ground

Preparation:

Cut the top of a pineapple and peel it using a sharp paring knife. Cut into small chunks and fill the measuring cup. Reserve the rest of the pineapple in a refrigerator.

Wash and trim off the beet. Cut into small slices and set aside.

Peel the orange and divide into wedges. Cut each wedge in half and set aside.

Now, combine pineapple, beet, and orange in a juicer and process until juiced. Transfer to a serving glass and stir in the coconut water and ginger.

Add some crushed ice and serve immediately.

Nutritional information per serving: Kcal: 135, Protein: 3.1g, Carbs: 40.7g, Fats: 0.5g

20. Kiwi Banana Juice

Ingredients:

3 whole kiwis, peeled

1 large banana, chopped

1 large strawberry, chopped

1 small apple, cored

¼ tsp of cinnamon, ground

Preparation:

Peel the kiwis and cut lengthwise in half. Set aside.

Peel the banana and chop into small chunks. Set aside.

Wash the strawberry and remove the stem. Cut into small pieces and set aside.

Wash the apple and cut in half. Remove the core and cut into bite-sized pieces. Set aside.

Now, combine kiwis, banana, strawberry, and apple in a juicer and process until juiced. Transfer to a serving glass and stir in the cinnamon.

Refrigerate for 10 minutes before serving.

Enjoy!

Nutritional information per serving: Kcal: 292, Protein: 4.4g, Carbs: 85g, Fats: 1.9g

21. Avocado Lemon Juice

Ingredients:

1 cup of avocado, cubed

1 whole lemon, peeled

1 cup of cranberries

1 cup of cucumber, sliced

1 cup of cherries, pitted

Preparation:

Peel the avocado and cut into small cubes. Fill the measuring cup and reserve the rest in the refrigerator. Set aside.

Peel the lemon and cut lengthwise in half. Set aside.

Wash the cranberries and set aside.

Wash the cucumber and cut into slices. Fill the measuring cup and reserve the the rest for later.

Wash the cherries and cut each in half. Remove the pits and set aside.

Now, combine avocado, cranberries, cucumber, and cherries in a juicer and process until juiced. Transfer to a serving glass and add some ice before serving.

Enjoy!

Nutritional information per serving: Kcal: 321, Protein: 5.8g, Carbs: 54.4g, Fats: 22.6g

22. Pomegranate Blackberry Juice

Ingredients:

1 cup of pomegranate seeds

1 cup of blackberries

1 whole lemon, peeled

1 medium-sized carrot, sliced

1 oz of water

Preparation:

Cut the top of the pomegranate fruit using a sharp paring knife. Slice down to each of the white membranes inside of the fruit. Pop the seeds into a measuring cup and set aside.

Wash the blackberries using a colander. Fill the measuring cup and reserve the rest. Set aside.

Peel the lemon and cut lengthwise in half. Set aside.

Wash and peel the carrot. Cut into thin slices and set aside.

Now, combine pomegranate seeds, blackberries, lemon, and carrot in a juicer. Process until juiced and transfer to a serving glass.

Add some ice or refrigerate for a while before serving.

Nutritional information per serving: Kcal: 119, Protein: 4.6g, Carbs: 41.3g, Fats: 2.1g

23. Celery Kale Juice

Ingredients:

1 cup of celery, chopped

1 cup of fresh kale, torn

1 cup of fresh mint, torn

1 whole lime, peeled

1 small Granny Smith's apple, cored

Preparation:

Wash the celery and chop into small pieces. Fill the measuring cup and set aside.

Combine kale and mint in a large colander. Wash thoroughly under cold running water. Slightly drain and torn with hands. Set aside.

Peel the lime and cut into small pieces. Set aside.

Wash the apple and cut in half. Remove the core and cut into bite-sized pieces. Set aside.

Now, combine celery, kale, mint, lime, and apple in a juicer and process until juiced. Transfer to a serving glass and add some ice before serving.

Enjoy!

Nutritional information per serving: Kcal: 121, Protein: 5.3g, Carbs: 35.8g, Fats: 1.3g

24. Potato Zucchini Juice

Ingredients:

1 cup of sweet potatoes, cubed

1 small zucchini, sliced

1 small apple, cored

¼ tsp of ginger, ground

Preparation:

Peel the sweet potato and cut into small cubes. Fill the measuring cup and reserve the rest for later.

Peel the zucchini and cut into thin slices. Set aside.

Wash the apple and cut in half. Remove the core and cut into bite-sized pieces. Set aside.

Now, combine sweet potatoes, zucchini, and apple in a juicer. Process until well juiced. Transfer to a serving glass and stir in the ginger.

Refrigerate for 10 minutes before serving.

Enjoy!

Nutritional information per serving: Kcal: 181, Protein: 4.2g, Carbs: 50.1g, Fats: 0.7g

25. Apricot Plum Juice

Ingredients:

2 whole apricots, pitted

2 whole plums, chopped

1 cup of cherries, pitted

1 small orange, peeled

1 tbsp of coconut water

Preparation:

Wash the apricots and cut in half. Remove the pits and cut all into small pieces. Set aside. Wash the plums and cut in half. Remove the pits and cut into bite-sized pieces. Set aside. Wash the cherries using a colander. Remove the pits and set aside. Peel the orange and divide into wedges. Cut each wedge in half and set aside. Now, combine apricots, plums, cherries, and orange in a juicer and process until well juiced. Transfer to a serving glass and stir in the coconut water.

Refrigerate for 10 minutes before serving.

Nutritional information per serving: Kcal: 191, Protein: 4.3g, Carbs: 56.3g, Fats: 1.1g

26. Fennel Broccoli Juice

Ingredients:

1 cup of fennel, chopped

1 cup of broccoli, chopped

1 cup of Brussels sprouts, halved

1 cup of watercress, torn

1 cup of cucumber, sliced

Preparation:

Wash the fennel and trim off the outer leaves. Using a sharp paring knife, cut into small pieces and fill the measuring cup. Reserve the rest for later.

Wash the broccoli and cut into small pieces. Fill the measuring cup and reserve the rest in the refrigerator. Set aside.

Wash the Brussels sprouts and trim off the outer layers. Cut in half and set aside.

Wash the watercress thoroughly under cold running water. Slightly drain and torn with hands. Set aside.

Wash the cucumber and cut into thin slices. Fill the

measuring cup and reserve the rest for later.

Now, combine fennel, broccoli, Brussels sprouts, watercress, and cucumber in a juicer and process until juiced. Transfer to a serving glass and refrigerate for 10 minutes before serving.

Enjoy!

Nutritional information per serving: Kcal: 72, Protein: 7.7g, Carbs: 22.6g, Fats: 0.8g

27. Cranberry Pear Juice

Ingredients:

1 cup of cranberries

1 medium-sized pear, chopped

1 whole lemon, peeled

½ cup of strawberries, sliced

1 small ginger knob, peeled

1 oz of water

Preparation:

Wash the cranberries and fill the measuring cup. Set aside.

Wash the pear and cut in half. Remove the core and cut into small pieces. Set aside.

Peel the lemon and cut in half. Set aside.

Wash the strawberries and remove the stems. Cut into small pieces and fill the measuring cup. Set aside.

Peel the ginger knob and set aside.

Now, combine cranberries, pear, lemon, strawberries, and ginger in a juicer and process until juiced. Transfer to a serving glass and stir in the water.

Serve cold.

Nutritional information per serving: Kcal: 143, Protein: 2.4g, Carbs: 52.7g, Fats: 0.8g

28. Beet Green Carrot Juice

Ingredients:

1 cup of beet greens, torn

1 large carrot, sliced

1 medium-sized orange, peeled

1 cup of cantaloupe, chopped

¼ tsp of ginger, ground

Preparation:

Wash the beet greens thoroughly under cold running water. Drain and torn with hands. Set aside.

Wash the carrot and cut into thin slices. Set aside.

Peel the orange and divide into wedges. Cut each wedge in half and set aside.

Cut the cantaloupe in half. Scoop out the seeds and cut one large wedge. Peel it and cut into small pieces. Fill the measuring cup and reserve the rest of the cantaloupe in a refrigerator.

Now, combine beet greens, carrot, orange, and cantaloupe in a juicer and process until juiced. Transfer to a serving glass and stir in the ginger.

Serve cold.

Nutritional information per serving: Kcal: 99, Protein: 3.5g, Carbs: 30.5g, Fats: 0.6g

29. Collard Greens Cucumber Juice

Ingredients:

2 cups of collard greens, chopped

1 cup of cucumber, sliced

1 whole lime, peeled

1 cup of Swiss chard, chopped

1 large celery stalk, chopped

1 oz of water

¼ tsp of salt

Preparation:

Combine collard greens and Swiss chard in a large colander. Wash it under running water and slightly drain. Chop into small pieces and set aside.

Wash the cucumber and cut into thin slices. Fill the measuring cup and reserve the rest in the refrigerator.

Peel the lime and cut lengthwise in half. Set aside.

Wash the celery and cut into small pieces. Set aside.

Now, combine collard greens, cucumber, lime, Swiss chard,

and celery in a juicer and process until juiced. Transfer to a serving glass and stir in the water and salt. Refrigerate for 10 minutes before serving.

Enjoy!

Nutritional information per serving: Kcal: 40, Protein: 3.8g, Carbs: 12.7g, Fats: 0.7g

30. Pumpkin Pepper Juice

Ingredients:

1 cup of pumpkin, cubed

1 large yellow bell pepper, chopped

1 small zucchini, sliced

¼ tsp of cinnamon, ground

Preparation:

Cut the pumpkin lengthwise in half. Scoop out the seeds and cut one large wedge. Peel it and fill the measuring cup. Wrap the rest of the pumpkin in a plastic foil and refrigerate for later.

Wash the bell pepper and cut in half. Remove the seeds and stem. Cut into bite-sized pieces and set aside.

Wash the zucchini thoroughly and cut into thin slices. Set aside.

Now, combine pumpkin, bell pepper, and zucchini in a juicer and process until juiced. Transfer to a serving glass and stir in the cinnamon.

Refrigerate for 10 minutes before serving.

Enjoy!

Nutritional information per serving: Kcal: 86, Protein: 4.5g, Carbs: 22.9g, Fats: 0.9g

31. Kale Celery Juice

Ingredients:

1 cup of fresh kale, chopped

2 medium-sized celery stalk, chopped

1 small apple, cored

1 cup of Romaine lettuce, shredded

Preparation:

Wash the kale thoroughly under cold running water. Slightly drain and chop it into small pieces. Set aside.

Wash the celery stalks and cut into bite-sized pieces. Set aside.

Wash the apple and cut in half. remove the core and cut into small pieces. Set aside.

Wash the lettuce leaves and shred it. Fill the measuring cup and reserve the rest for later.

Now, combine kale, celery, apple, and lettuce in a juicer and process until juiced. Transfer to a serving glass and add some ice before serving.

Enjoy!

Nutritional information per serving: Kcal: 103, Protein: 4.6g, Carbs: 29.4g, Fats: 1.2g

32. Melon Lime Juice

Ingredients:

1 medium-sized wedge of honeydew melon

1 whole lime, peeled

1 small Granny Smith's apple, cored

1 large banana, peeled

¼ tsp of cinnamon, ground

Preparation:

Cut one large honeydew melon wedge and peel it. Remove the seeds and cut into bite-sized pieces. Wrap the rest of the melon in a plastic foil and refrigerate.

Peel the lime and cut lengthwise in half. Set aside.

Wash the apple and cut in half. Remove the core and cut into bite-sized pieces. Set aside.

Peel the banana and chop into small chunks. Set aside.

Now, combine melon, lime, apple, and banana in a juicer and process until juiced. Transfer to a serving glass and stir in the cinnamon.

Refrigerate for 10 minutes before serving.

Nutritional information per serving: Kcal: 226, Protein: 4.6g, Carbs: 29.4g, Fats: 1.2g

33. Guava Cherry Juice

Ingredients:

1 whole guava, peeled

1 cup of cherries, pitted

1 medium-sized orange, wedged

1 whole apricot, pitted

Preparation:

Peel the guava and cut into small chunks. Set aside.

Wash the cherries using a colander. Remove the stems and cut each in half. Remove the pits and fill the measuring cup. Set aside.

Peel the orange and divide into wedges. Cut each wedge in half and set aside.

Wash the apricot and cut in half. Remove the pit and cut into bite-sized pieces. Set aside.

Now, combine guava, cherries, orange, and apricot in a juicer and process until juiced. Transfer to a serving glass and add some ice.

Serve immediately.

Nutritional information per serving: Kcal: 173, Protein: 4.7g, Carbs: 51.8g, Fats: 1.1g

34. Mango Kiwi Juice

Ingredients:

1 cup of mango, chunked

1 whole kiwi, peeled

1 cup of fresh spinach, chopped

1 small ginger knob, peeled

2 tbsp of coconut water

Preparation:

Peel the mango and cut into small chunks. Fill the measuring cup and reserve the rest in the refrigerator.

Peel the kiwi and cut lengthwise in half. Set aside.

Wash the spinach thoroughly under cold running water. Slightly drain and chop it into small pieces. Set aside.

Peel the ginger knob and set aside.

Now, combine mango, kiwi, spinach, and ginger in a juicer and process until juiced. Transfer to a serving glass and stir in the coconut water. Refrigerate for 10 minutes before serving.

Enjoy!

Nutritional information per serving: Kcal: 190, Protein: 9.1g, Carbs: 53.6g, Fats: 2.2g

35. Pomegranate Plum Juice

Ingredients:

1 cup of pomegranate seeds

2 whole plums, pitted

1 small Golden Delicious apple, cored

1 large strawberry, chopped

Preparation:

Cut the top of the pomegranate fruit using a sharp paring knife. Slice down to each of the white membranes inside of the fruit. Pop the seeds into a measuring cup and set aside.

Wash the plums and cut lengthwise in half. Remove the pits and cut into small pieces. Set aside.

Wash the apple and cut in half. Remove the core and cut into bite-sized pieces. Set aside.

Wash the strawberry and remove the stem. Cut into small pieces and set aside.

Now, combine pomegranate seeds, plums, apple, and strawberry in a juicer and process until juiced. Transfer to a serving glass and add some crushed ice.

Serve immediately.

Nutritional information per serving: Kcal: 176, Protein: 2.8g, Carbs: 50.3g, Fats: 1.6g

36. Watermelon Cranberry Juice

Ingredients:

1 cup of watermelon, chopped

1 cup of whole cranberries

1 whole lemon, peeled

1 cup of fresh mint, chopped

1 tbsp of liquid honey

Preparation:

Cut the watermelon lengthwise. For one cup, you will need a large slice. Peel and cut into chunks. Remove the seeds and set aside. Reserve the rest for some other juices.

Wash the cranberries using a colander. Fill the measuring cup and reserve the rest in the refrigerator.

Peel the lemon and cut lengthwise in half. Set aside.

Wash the mint thoroughly under cold running water and roughly chop it. Set aside.

Now, combine watermelon, cranberries, lemon, and mint in a juicer and process until juiced. Transfer to a serving glass and stir in the honey.

Add few ice cubes and serve immediately.

Enjoy!

Nutritional information per serving: Kcal: 93, Protein: 2.9g, Carbs: 32.8g, Fats: 0.7g

37. Grape Pineapple Juice

Ingredients:

1 cup of black grapes

1 cup of pineapple, chunked

1 tsp of vanilla extract

Preparation:

In a heavy-bottomed pot, combine grapes and one cup of water. Bring it to a boil over a medium-high temperature, stirring occasionally. Stir in the vanilla extract and remove from the heat. Set aside to cool completely.

Cut the top of a pineapple fruit. Using a sharp paring knife, peel it and cut into thin slices. Fill the measuring cup and reserve the rest for later.

Now, combine grape mixture and pineapple in a juicer and process until well juiced. Transfer to a serving glass and refrigerate for 20 minutes before serving.

Garnish with some fresh mint, but it's optional.

Enjoy!

Nutritional information per serving: Kcal: 200, Protein: 2.1g, Carbs: 57g, Fats: 0.8g

38. Tomato Celery Juice

Ingredients:

5 cherry tomatoes, halved

1 large celery stalk, chopped

1 cup of cucumber, sliced

1 cup of fresh parsley, chopped

¼ tsp of salt

¼ tsp of black pepper, ground

½ tsp of Tabasco sauce

1 oz of water

Preparation:

Wash the cherry tomatoes and remove the stems. Cut each tomato in half and set aside.

Wash the celery stalk and chop it into bite-sized pieces. Set aside.

Wash the cucumber and cut into thin slices. Fill the measuring cup and reserve the rest for later.

Place the parsley in a colander and rinse it thoroughly.

Slightly drain and chop into small pieces. Set aside.

Now, combine cherry tomatoes, celery, cucumber, and parsley in a juicer and process until juiced. Transfer to a serving glass and stir in the salt, pepper, Tabasco sauce, and water.

Serve immediately!

Nutritional information per serving: Kcal: 38, Protein: 3.3g, Carbs: 10.9g, Fats: 0.8g

39. Blueberry Ginger Juice

Ingredients:

2 cups of blueberries

1 small ginger knob, peeled and chopped

1 medium-sized blood orange, peeled

1 cup of black grapes

Preparation:

Place the blueberries in a colander. Wash thoroughly under cold running water and drain. Fill the measuring cups and reserve the rest in the freezer.

Peel the ginger and cut into small pieces. Set aside.

Peel the orange and divide into wedges. Cut each wedge in half and set aside.

Wash the grapes and fill the measuring cup. Set aside.

Now, combine blueberries, ginger, orange, and grapes in a juicer and process until juiced. Transfer to a serving glass and add few ice cubes before serving.

Nutritional information per serving: Kcal: 254, Protein: 4.1g, Carbs: 75.2g, Fats: 1.5g

40. Avocado Papaya Juice

Ingredients:

1 cup of avocado, cubed

1 small papaya, chopped

1 cup of cherries, halved

1 whole lemon, peeled

¼ tsp of cinnamon, ground

1 oz of water

Preparation:

Peel the avocado and cut lengthwise in half. Remove the pit and cut into small cubes. Fill the measuring cup and reserve the rest for later.

Peel the papaya and cut into small chunks. Set aside.

Peel the lemon and cut lengthwise in half. Set aside.

Now, combine avocado, papaya, and lemon in a juicer and process until juiced. Transfer to a serving glass and stir in the cinnamon and water.

Refrigerate for 15 minutes before serving and enjoy!

Nutritional information per serving: Kcal: 343, Protein: 5.8g, Carbs: 57.3g, Fats: 22.8g

41. Pumpkin Apple Juice

Ingredients:

1 cup of pumpkin, cubed

1 small Granny Smith's apple, cored

1 medium-sized carrot, sliced

1 cup of cucumber, sliced

¼ tsp of cinnamon, ground

¼ tsp of ginger, ground

Preparation:

Cut the pumpkin in half and scoop out the seeds. Wash it and cut one large wedge. Peel it and cut into small cubes. Fill the measuring cup and reserve the rest in the refrigerator.

Wash the apple and cut lengthwise in half. Remove the core and cut into small pieces. Set aside.

Wash and peel the carrot. Cut into thin slices and set aside.

Wash the cucumber and cut into thin slices. Fill the measuring cup and reserve the rest for later.

Now, combine pumpkin, apple, carrot, and cucumber in a

juicer and process until juiced. Transfer to a serving glass and stir in the cinnamon and ginger.

Refrigerate for 10 minutes before serving.

Nutritional information per serving: Kcal: 121, Protein: 2.7g, Carbs: 34.8g, Fats: 0.6g

42. Peach Lime Juice

Ingredients:

2 large peaches, pitted

1 whole lime, peeled

1 cup of apricots, sliced

1 large banana, peeled

Preparation:

Wash the peaches and cut in half. Remove the pits and cut each half into bite-sized pieces. Set aside.

Peel the lime and roughly chop it. Make sure to reserve lime juice while cutting.

Wash the apricots and cut in half. Remove the pits and cut into small pieces. Fill the measuring cup and set aside.

Peel the banana and cut into small chunks. Set aside.

Now, combine peaches, lime, apricots, and banana in a juicer and process until juiced. Transfer to a serving glass and add some crushed ice before serving.

Enjoy!

Nutritional information per serving: Kcal: 299, Protein: 7.2g, Carbs: 86.5g, Fats: 2g

43. Artichoke Spinach Juice

Ingredients:

1 medium-sized artichoke, chopped

1 cup of fresh spinach, chopped

1 cup of green beans, chopped

1 small green bell pepper, sliced

1 small ginger knob, peeled and sliced

Preparation:

Trim off the outer leaves of the artichoke using a sharp paring knife. Wash it and cut into bite-sized pieces. Set aside.

Using a colander, rinse the spinach thoroughly under cold running water. Chop into small pieces and set aside.

Place the beans in a deep pot. Add 1 cup of water and bring it to a boil. Cook for 5 minutes and remove from the heat. Set aside to cool completely.

Wash the bell pepper and cut in half. Remove the seeds and stem. Cut into small rings and set aside.

Peel the ginger knob and chop it into small pieces. Set

aside.

Now, combine artichoke, spinach, green beans, bell pepper, and ginger in a juicer and process until juiced. Transfer to a serving glass and refrigerate for 10 minutes before serving.

Nutritional information per serving: Kcal: 95, Protein: 11.9g, Carbs: 29.4g, Fats: 1.3g

44. Orange Pear Juice

Ingredients:

1 medium-sized orange, peeled

1 medium-sized pear, chopped

1 whole plum, pitted

1 whole lemon, peeled

1 oz of water

Preparation:

Peel the orange and divide into wedges. Cut each wedge in half and set aside.

Wash the pear and cut in half. Remove the core and chop into small pieces. Set aside.

Wash the plum and cut in half. Remove the pit and cut in small pieces.

Peel the lemon and cut into quarters. Set aside.

Now, combine orange, pear, plum, and lemon in a juicer and process until juiced. Transfer to a serving glass and stir in the water.

You can add a pinch of minced mint for some extra smooth

flavor, but it's optional.

Add some crushed ice and serve immediately.

Nutritional information per serving: Kcal: 166, Protein: 2.9g, Carbs: 55.4g, Fats: 0.8g

45. Carrot Grapefruit Juice

Ingredients:

2 medium-sized carrots, sliced

1 whole grapefruit, wedged

1 cup of Romaine lettuce, shredded

1 cup of fresh mint, chopped

1 whole lime, peeled

Preparation:

Wash and peel the carrots. Cut into thin slices and set aside.

Peel the grapefruit and divide into wedges. Cut each wedge in half and set aside.

Wash the lettuce thoroughly under cold running water. Shred it and fill the measuring cup. Reserve the rest for later.

Wash the mint and then place it in a medium bowl. Add one cup of hot water and let it soak for 10 minutes. Slightly drain and set aside.

Peel the lime and cut lengthwise in half. Set aside.

Now, combine carrots, grapefruit, lettuce, mint, and lime in a juicer and process until juiced. Transfer to a serving glass and add some crushed ice before serving.

Enjoy!

Nutritional information per serving: Kcal: 147, Protein: 4.7g, Carbs: 46.8g, Fats: 1.1g

46. Swiss Chard Juice

Ingredients:

2 cups of Swiss chard, chopped

1 cup of fresh kale, chopped

1 cup of collard greens, chopped

1 whole lemon, peeled

1 cup of cucumber, sliced

¼ tsp of ginger, ground

Preparation:

Combine Swiss chard, kale, and collard greens in a large colander. Wash thoroughly under cold running water. Slightly drain and roughly chop all. Set aside.

Peel the lemon and cut lengthwise in half. Set aside.

Wash the cucumber and cut into thin slices. Fill the measuring cup and reserve the rest in the refrigerator. Set aside.

Now, combine Swiss chard, kale, collard greens, lemon, and cucumber in a juicer. Process until juiced.

Transfer to a serving glass and stir in the ginger.

Serve cold.

Nutritional information per serving: Kcal: 57, Protein: 6.3g, Carbs: 17.8g, Fats: 1.2g

47. Broccoli Brussels Sprout Juice

Ingredients:

1 cup of broccoli, chopped

1 cup of Brussels sprouts, halved

1 cup of cucumber, sliced

1 whole lime, peeled

¼ tsp of ginger, ground

Preparation:

Wash the broccoli and trim off the outer layers. Cut into small pieces and fill the measuring cup. Set aside.

Wash the Brussels sprouts and trim off the outer leaves. Cut each sprout in half and fill the measuring cup. Reserve the rest for in the refrigerator.

Wash the cucumber and cut into thin slices. Fill the measuring cup and reserve the rest for later. Set aside.

Peel the lime and cut lengthwise in half.

Now, combine broccoli, Brussels sprouts, cucumber, and lime in a juicer and process until juiced. Transfer to a serving glass and stir in the ginger.

Add few ice cubes and serve immediately.

Nutritional information per serving: Kcal: 63, Protein: 6.1g, Carbs: 19.5g, Fats: 1.2g

48. Blackberry Avocado Juice

Ingredients:

2 cups of blackberries

1 cup of avocado, cubed

1 medium-sized apple, cored

¼ tsp of ginger, ground

Preparation:

Place the blackberries in a colander and wash thoroughly under cold running water. Slightly drain and set aside.

Peel the avocado and cut lengthwise in half. Remove the pit and cut into small cubes. Fill the measuring cup and reserve the rest in the refrigerator.

Wash the apple and cut in half. Remove the core and cut into bite-sized pieces. Set aside.

Now, combine blackberries, avocado, and apple in a juicer and process until juiced. Transfer to a serving glass and stir in the ginger.

Add some ice and serve immediately.

Nutritional information per serving: Kcal: 342, Protein: 7.7g, Carbs: 63.2g, Fats: 23.7g

49. Raspberry Pear Juice

Ingredients:

1 cup of raspberries

1 large pear, chopped

1 whole lemon, peeled

1 small green apple, cored

Preparation:

Wash the raspberries thoroughly using a colander. Slightly drain and set aside.

Wash the pear and cut in half. Remove the core and cut into bite-sized pieces. Set aside.

Peel the lemon and cut lengthwise in half. Set aside.

Wash the apple and cut in half. Remove the core and cut into small pieces. Set aside.

Now, combine raspberries, pear, lemon, and apple in a juicer and process until juiced. Transfer to a serving glass and add some ice before serving.

Enjoy!

Nutritional information per serving: Kcal: 214, Protein: 3.6g, Carbs: 74.7g, Fats: 1.6g

50. Coco Squash Juice

Ingredients:

1 cup of crookneck squash, sliced

1 medium-sized pear, chopped

1 cup of cucumber, sliced

1 whole lime, peeled

1 oz of coconut water

Preparation:

Peel the crookneck squash and scrape out the seeds with a spoon. Cut into small cubes and fill the measuring cup. Reserve the rest of the squash for some other recipe. Wrap in a plastic foil and refrigerate.

Wash the pear and cut in half. Remove the core and chop into small pieces. Set aside.

Wash the cucumber and cut into thin slices. Fill the measuring cup and reserve the rest in the refrigerator. Set aside.

Peel the lime and cut lengthwise in half. Set aside.

Now, combine squash, pear, cucumber, and lime in a juicer.

Process until juiced. Transfer to a serving glass and stir in the coconut water.

Add some ice and serve immediately.

Nutritional information per serving: Kcal: 120, Protein: 2.4g, Carbs: 37.6g, Fats: 0.7g

51. Kiwi Papaya Juice

Ingredients:

4 whole kiwis, peeled

2 small papaya, chopped

1 tbsp of fresh basil, roughly chopped

1 large banana, peeled

1 cup of cucumber, sliced

Preparation:

Peel the kiwis and cut in half. Set aside.

Peel the papaya and cut in half. Remove the seeds and dice into small pieces. Set aside.

Peel the banana and cut into chunks. Set aside.

Wash the cucumber and cut into thin slices. Fill the measuring cup and reserve the rest for later. Set aside.

Now, combine kiwis, papaya, basil, banana, and cucumber in a juicer and process until juiced. Transfer to a serving glass and add some ice before serving.

Enjoy!

Nutritional information per serving: Kcal: 365, Protein: 6.5g, Carbs: 107g, Fats: 2.8g

52. Pepper Broccoli Juice

Ingredients:

1 large red bell pepper, chopped

1 cup of broccoli, chopped

1 cup of cucumber, sliced

1 large celery stalk, chopped

¼ tsp of ginger, ground

Preparation:

Wash the pepper and cut in half. Remove the seeds and stem. Cut into thin slices and set aside.

Wash the broccoli and trim off the outer wilted layers. Cut into small pieces and set aside.

Wash the cucumber and cut into thin slices. Fill the measuring cup and reserve the rest in the refrigerator.

Wash the celery stalk and cut into small pieces. Set aside.

Now, combine pepper, broccoli, cucumber, and celery in a juicer and process until well juiced. Transfer to a serving glass and stir in the ginger.

Refrigerate for 10 minutes before serving.

Nutritional information per serving: Kcal: 71, Protein: 4.9g, Carbs: 19.7g, Fats: 1g

53. Cantaloupe Orange Juice

Ingredients:

1 cup of cantaloupe, diced

1 small orange, peeled

1 cup of fresh mint, torn

1 whole lemon, peeled

¼ tsp of ginger, ground

Preparation:

Cut the cantaloupe in half. Scoop out the seeds and cut one medium wedge. Peel it and dice into small pieces. Reserve the rest of the cantaloupe in a refrigerator.

Peel the orange and divide into wedges. Cut each wedge in half and set aside.

Wash the mint thoroughly under cold water. Slightly drain and torn with hands. Set aside.

Peel the lemon and cut lengthwise in half. Set aside.

Now, combine cantaloupe, orange, mint, and lemon in a juicer and process until juiced. Transfer to a serving glass and stir in the ginger.

Add some ice before serving and enjoy!

Nutritional information per serving: Kcal: 104, Protein: 3.8g, Carbs: 33.2g, Fats: 0.8g

54. Tomato Greens Juice

Ingredients:

7 cherry tomatoes, halved

2 cups of Swiss chard, torn

2 cups of collard greens, torn

1 cup of cucumber, sliced

1 whole leek, chopped

Preparation:

Wash the tomatoes and remove the stems. Cut each tomato in half and set aside.

Combine Swiss chard and collard greens in a large colander. Wash thoroughly under cold running water. Slightly drain and torn with hands. Set aside.

Wash the cucumber and cut into thin slices. Fill the measuring cup and reserve the rest for later.

Wash the leek and cut into small pieces. Set aside.

Now, combine tomatoes, Swiss chard, collard greens, cucumber, and leek in a juicer and process until juiced. Transfer to a serving glass and refrigerate for 10 minutes before serving.

Nutritional information per serving: Kcal: 91, Protein: 6.2g, Carbs: 25.7g, Fats: 1.1g

55. Mango Citrus Juice

Ingredients:

1 cup of mango, chunked

1 whole lemon, peeled

1 whole lime, peeled

1 small green apple, cored

1 tbsp of coconut water

¼ tsp of cinnamon, ground

Preparation:

Peel the mango and cut into small chunks. Fill the measuring cup and reserve the rest for later.

Peel the lemon and lime. Cut each fruit in half and set aside.

Wash the apple and cut in half. Remove the core and cut into bite-sized pieces. Set aside.

Now, combine mango, lemon, lime, and apple in a juicer and process until juiced. Transfer to a serving glass and stir in the coconut water and cinnamon.

Add some crushed ice and serve immediately.

Nutritional information per serving: Kcal: 178, Protein: 2.8g, Carbs: 53.4g, Fats: 1.1g

56. Beet Kale Juice

Ingredients:

1 whole beet, sliced

1 cup of fresh kale, torn

1 small green apple, cored

1 small orange, peeled

¼ tsp of ginger, ground

Preparation:

Wash and trim off the beet. Slightly peel and cut into thin slices. Set aside.

Place the kale in a colander and wash under running water. Drain and torn with hands. Set aside.

Wash the apple and cut in half. Remove the core and cut into bite-sized pieces. Set aside.

Peel the orange and divide into wedges. Cut each wedge in half and set aside.

Now, combine beet, kale, apple, and orange in a juicer and process until juiced. Transfer to a serving glass and stir in the ginger.

Add some crushed ice and serve immediately.

Nutritional information per serving: Kcal: 153, Protein: 5.7g, Carbs: 44.6g, Fats: 1.1g

57. Blueberry Kiwi Juice

Ingredients:

1 cup of blueberries

2 whole kiwis, peeled

1 whole lemon, peeled

1 cup of cantaloupe, diced

1 tbsp of coconut water

Preparation:

Place the blueberries in a colander. Wash thoroughly and drain. Set aside.

Peel the kiwis and lemon. Cut lengthwise in half and set aside.

Cut the cantaloupe in half. Scoop out the seeds and cut one large wedge. Peel it and cut into small pieces. Fill the measuring cup and reserve the rest of the cantaloupe in a refrigerator.

Now, combine blueberries, kiwis, lemon, and cantaloupe in a juicer and process until juiced. Transfer to a serving glass and stir in the coconut water.

Refrigerate for 10 minutes before serving.

Nutritional information per serving: Kcal: 196, Protein: 4.6g, Carbs: 59.8g, Fats: 1.6g

SALAD RECIPES

1. Buddha Bowl Salad

Ingredients:

½ cup drained chickpeas

¼ sliced avocado

½ sliced cucumber

1 cup baby spinach

1 sliced carrot

½ cup sliced radish

1 tbsp olive oil

Salt and pepper to taste

Preparation:

Rinse the chickpeas under running water using a colander. Drain and set aside.

Peel the avocado and cut lengthwise in half. Remove the pit and peel. Cut one half into two equal halves and thinly slice it. Set aside.

Rinse the baby spinach under running water and drain. Cut into small pieces and set aside.

Wash and peel the carrot. Cut into thin slices and set aside.

Now, combine all ingredients in a salad bowl and drizzle with olive oil, salt, and pepper.

Serve immediately.

Nutritional information per serving: Kcal: 451, Protein: 10.2g, Carbs: 38.9g, Fats: 26.4g

2.   Egg Pepper Salad

Ingredients:

1 cup red bell pepper, chopped

4 large eggs

1 small tomato, chopped

1 tbsp olive oil

1 tsp balsamic vinegar

1 tbsp corn

Salt and pepper

Preparation:

Place the eggs in a heavy-bottomed pot and add water enough to cover. Bring to a boil and cook for 10 minutes. Using a slotted spoon, remove the eggs from the water and transfer to a bowl filled with ice cold water. Peel and chop into bite-sized pieces. Transfer to a large salad bowl and set aside.

Wash the tomato and chop into bite-sized pieces. Add to the bowl along with corn. Sprinkle all with olive oil, balsamic vinegar, salt, and pepper.

Stir until well combined and serve immediately.

Enjoy!

Nutritional information per serving: Kcal: 297, Protein: 16.1g, Carbs: 21.6g, Fats: 18.1g

3.   Tuna Spinach Salad with Tomatoes and Onion

Ingredients:

2 cups canned tuna, drained

2 cups baby spinach, chopped

1 tomato, chopped

1 large onion, thinly sliced

1 tbsp olive oil

½ tsp dried thyme, ground

Salt and pepper to taste

Preparation:

Using a large colander, rinse the spinach under running water. Drain and chop into small pieces. Place in a large salad bowl and set aside.

Wash the tomato and chop into bite-sized pieces. Set aside.

Peel the onion and cut into thin slices. Set aside.

Now, combine spinach, tomatoes, and onion. Top with tuna and sprinkle all with thyme, salt, and pepper. Mix until well combined.

Refrigerate for 10-15 minutes before serving.

Nutritional information per serving: Kcal: 310, Protein: 47.4g, Carbs: 9.5g, Fats: 8.7g

4. Feta Beans Salad

Ingredients:

½ cup Feta cheese, crumbled

½ cup canned red beans, drained

1 cup Iceberg lettuce, torn

1 small red onion, chopped

1 small carrot, slices

1 tbsp olive oil

1 tbsp lime juice, freshly squeezed

Preparation:

Rinse the lettuce under running water. Drain and torn with your hands into small pieces. Place in a large salad bowl and set aside.

Peel the onion and slices into thin slices.

Rinse the carrot and trim off the ends. Cut into thin slices and set aside.

In a small mixing bowl, combine olive oil, lime juice, salt, and pepper. Optionally, add some cayenne pepper for some spicy aroma. Mix until well combined and set aside.

Now, combine all ingredients in a salad bowl and drizzle with previously prepared dressing. Mix and serve immediately

Enjoy!

Nutritional information per serving: Kcal: 342, Protein: 16.4g, Carbs: 36.3g, Fats: 15.6g

5. Creamy Spinach Salad

Ingredients:

2 cups spinach, choppe

¼ cup low-fat yogurt

1 garlic clove, minced

1 tbsp olive oil

¼ tsp cayenne pepper, ground

¼ tsp sea salt

Preparation:

Using a large colander, rinse the spinach thoroughly under running water. Drain and chop into small pieces.

Transfer the spinach into a steam basket. Pour 2 cups of water in a deep pot. Bring to a boil and place the steam basket on top of the pot. Steam for 10 minutes, or until the spinach has been completely wilted. Set aside.

In a small bowl, combine yogurt, garlic, olive oil, cayenne pepper, and salt. Mix until combined and set aside.

Now, transfer spinach to a serving dish and drizzle with previously prepared dressing. Mix and serve immediately.

Enjoy!

Nutritional information per serving: Kcal: 183, Protein: 5.5g, Carbs: 7.7g, Fats: 15.1g

6. Spicy Chickpea Salad

Ingredients:

1 cup canned chickpeas, drained and rinsed

1 small chili pepper, chopped

1 small red onion, chopped

1 medium-sized tomato, chopped

1 tbsp olive oil

1 tsp yellow mustard

Salt and pepper to taste

Preparation:

Using a small colander, rinse well the chickpeas. Drain and transfer to a large salad bowl. Set aside.

Cut the chili pepper lengthwise in half and remove the seeds. Chop into small pieces and set aside.

Peel the onion and chop into small pieces. Set aside.

Rinse the tomato and chop into bite-sized pieces. Set aside.

In a small bowl, combine oil, mustard, salt, and pepper. Mix until combined.

In a large bowl with chickpeas, add all the remaining ingredients. Drizzle all with oil mixture and give it a good stir.

Serve immediately.

Nutritional information per serving: Kcal: 301, Protein: 13.6g, Carbs: 44.4g, Fats: 8.9g

7. Warm Mushroom Rice Salad

Ingredients:

2 cups button mushrooms, sliced

½ cup brown rice

1 large tomato, chopped

1 tbsp fresh parsley, finely chopped

1 tbsp lime juice, freshly squeezed

1 tbsp olive oil

Salt and pepper

Preparation:

Place the rice in a heavy-bottomed pot. Add 1 cup of water and bring it to a boil. Reduce the heat to low and cook for 10-15 minutes, or until almost all the liquid has been evaporated. Remove from the heat and set let it chill for a while.

Meanwhile, wash the mushrooms and chop into small pieces. Set aside.

Preheat the oil in a nonstick skillet over a medium-high heat. Add mushrooms and cook for 4-5 minutes, or until all the liquid has been evaporated. Remove from the heat and set aside.

Now, combine previously cooked rice and mushrooms. Add chopped tomato, and parsley. Mix until well combined and sprinkle all with salt, pepper, and lime juice.

Stir once and serve immediately.

Nutritional information per serving: Kcal: 264, Protein: 6.6g, Carbs: 42.1g, Fats: 8.7g

8. Egg Almond Creme Salad

Ingredients:

5 large eggs

½ cup almonds, grated

1 cup cherry tomatoes, chopped

1 cup Greek yogurt

1 tbsp lemon juice

1 tbsp flaxseeds

Salt and pepper

Preparation:

Place the eggs in a deep pot and cover with water. Bring to a boil and then cook for 10-12 minutes. Remove immediately from the pot and transfer to a bowl with ice cold water. Let it chill for 2 minutes and peel.

Transfer the eggs to a food processor and add Greek yogurt, lemon juice, flaxseeds, salt, and pepper. Pulse until smooth and creamy.

Transfer the egg mixture to a serving bowl and top with grated almonds.

Refrigerate for at least 20 minutes before serving.

Enjoy!

Nutritional information per serving: Kcal: 285, Protein: 21.6g, Carbs: 9.8g, Fats: 18.4g

9. Carrot Lentil Salad

Ingredients:

4 large carrots, sliced

1 cup Greek yogurt

½ cup canned lentils

1 cup Iceberg lettuce, chopped

1 tbsp olive oil

1 tsp apple cider vinegar

Salt

Preparation:

Place the lentils in a colander and rinse under running water. Drain well and set aside.

Slightly peel the carrots and trim off the green ends. Cut into thin slices and set aside.

In a small bowl, combine Greek yogurt, olive oil, apple cider vinegar, and salt. Mix until combined and set aside.

In a large bowl, combine carrots, lentils, and lettuce. Drizzle all with yogurt mixture and give it a good stir. Refrigerate for 30 minutes before serving.

Enjoy!

Nutritional information per serving: Kcal: 368, Protein: 23.8g, Carbs: 47.9g, Fats: 9.6g

10. Couscous Salad

Ingredients:

¼ cup couscous

¼ eggplant, chopped

1 cup button mushrooms, sliced

¼ avocado, sliced

½ red bell pepper, chopped

1 cup broccoli

1 tbsp sesame oil

2 tbsp soy sauce

1 tsp mirin

¼ tsp salt

Preparation:

Place couscous in a pot and pour in enough water to barely cover. Stir well, sprinkle with salt, and bring to a boil. Reduce the heat to medium-low and cook for about 10 minutes. When done, remove from the heat and fluff with a fork. Cool for a while.

Meanwhile, grease a large wok pan with sesame oil and heat up. Add eggplant and broccoli. Sprinkle with salt and cook for 5-6 minutes

Now, add mushrooms, avocado, and red pepper. Sprinkle with mirin, soy sauce, and some more salt. Give it a good stir and continue to cook for 3-4 minutes

Finally, stir in couscous and cook for 2-3 more minutes.

Serve immediately.

Nutritional information per serving: Kcal: 504, Protein: 15.1g, Carbs: 61.9g, Fats: 24g

11. Grilled Peach Salad with Goat's Cheese

Ingredients:

1 sliced peach

1 cup baby spinach

1 cup arugula

3/4 cup goat's cheese

1 tsp coconut oil,

1 tbsp agave nectar

2 tbsp chopped walnuts

Preparation:

Preheat the grill to high heat.

Rinse the spinach thoroughly under running water. Drain and chop into small pieces. Set aside.

Slice peach into half-inch thick slices and brush with coconut oil.

Grill for 2-3 minutes on each side and transfer to a plate. Add the remaining ingredients and drizzle with agave nectar.

Toss to combine and serve immediately.

Nutritional information per serving: Kcal: 315, Protein: 12.5g, Carbs: 19g, Fats: 23g

12.   French Beans Salad

Ingredients:

7 oz cooked french beans

1 cup sweet potato chunks

½ purple onion

½ sliced tomato

½ sliced carrot

1 chopped green chili

1 cup vegetable stock

1 tbsp oil

½ tsp curry powder

1 tsp cumin seeds

Salt and pepper to taste

Preparation:

Peel the potatoes and cut into small chunks. Reserve the rest in the refrigerator.

Peel the onion and cut into thin slices. Set aside.

Wash the tomato and chop into bite-sized pieces. Set aside.

Cut the chili lengthwise in half. Remove the seeds and chop into small pieces. Set aside.

Heat the oil in a large pan over medium-high heat. Add onions and carrots and cook for 4-5 minutes, stirring constantly.

Now, add green chili, tomato, cumin seeds, curry powder, salt, and pepper. Give it a good stir and continue to cook for 4-5 minutes. Finally, add the remaining ingredients and cook for 2 more minutes

Remove from the heat and let it cool completely before serving.

Nutritional information per serving: Kcal: 580, Protein: 9g, Carbs: 68.2g, Fats: 29.5g

13. Portobello Rice Salad

Ingredients:

½ cup rice

3 sliced Portobello mushrooms

1 tbsp sesame oil

2 tbsp soy sauce

½ tbsp sesame seeds

1 tsp honey

1 tbsp chopped parsley leaves

Salt and pepper to taste

Preparation:

Place rice in a heavy-bottomed pot and pour in 1 1/2 cup of water. Season with some salt and bring it to a boil. Reduce the heat to medium-low and simmer until all the liquid has evaporated. Stir occasionally.

When done, remove the rice from the heat and set aside.

Meanwhile, grease a non-stick skillet with some oil and heat up over medium-high heat. Add sliced mushrooms and season with salt and pepepr. Cook for 7-8 minutes, stirring occasionally.

Now add soy sauce, sesame seeds, honey, and parsley. Stir in the rice and continue to cook for 2 more minutes.

Remove from the heat and serve.

Nutritional information per serving: Kcal: 583, Protein: 18g, Carbs: 92g, Fats: 16g

14. Quinoa Salad with Grilled Cauliflower

Ingredients:

¼ cup quinoa

1 cup cauliflower florets

1 cup broccoli

½ sliced green pepper

1 cup cherry tomatoes

1 cup arugula

½ chopped purple onion

1 tbsp oil

½ tsp apple cider vinegar

Salt and to taste

Preparation:

Place quinoa in a fine mesh sieve and rinse well under cold running water. Transfer to a small saucepan and pour in 1/2 cup of water. Bring it to a boil and reduce the heat to low. Cook for 10 minutes, stirring constantly. Remove from the heat and cool. Set aside.

Now, brush a small grill pan with some oil and heat up over high heat. Add cauliflower and broccoli, sprinkle with some salt, and cook until tender and lightly charred. Remove from the heat and transfer to a bowl.

Stir in cooked quinoa and add vegetables. Sprinkle with oil, apple cider, and some salt to taste.

Serve immediately.

Nutritional information per serving: Kcal: 404, Protein: 14.3g, Carbs: 53.8g, Fats: 17.3g

15. Sweet Broccoli Salad

Ingredients:

1 cup broccoli florets

½ chopped tomato

1 cup chopped kale

½ cup shredded cabbage

2 tbsp chopped almonds

1 sliced orange,

2 tbsp agave nectar

¼ tsp ginger powder

Preparation:

Rinse the broccoli florets using a large colander. Drain and transfer to a large pot. Add water enough to cover and bring to a boil over medium-high heat. Cook for 5 minutes. Remove from the heat and drain well. Set aside.

Combine kale and cabbage in a large colander. Rinse well and drain. Chop into small pieces and set aside.

In a large bowl, combine tomatoes, kale, cabbage, orange, and broccoli. Top with almonds, agave nectar, and ginger.

Serve immediately.

Nutritional information per serving: Kcal: 294, Protein: 9.2g, Carbs: 55.9g, Fats: 6.4g

16. Asparagus Rice Salad with Lime

Ingredients:

¼ cup rice

3.5oz chopped asparagus

½ sliced cucumber

¼ cup drained green peas

1 tbsp sesame oil

2 tbsp freshly squeezed lime juice

Salt and pepper to taste

Preparation:

Place rice in a heavy-bottomed pot and pour in 3/4 cup of water. Sprinkle with some salt and bring it to a boil. Reduce the heat to medium and cook for 7-10 minutes, or until all the liquid has evaporated. Remove from the heat and cool to a room temperature. Set aside.

Grease a large skillet with oil and heat up over medium-high heat. Add asparagus and cook for 3-4 minutes, stirring constantly.

Now, add peas and season with some salt and pepper to

taste. Continue to cook for 2 minutes. Remove from the heat and transfer to a bowl. Stir in the chilled rice and add sliced cucumber.

Sprinkle with lime juice and serve immediately.

Nutritional information per serving: Kcal: 368, Protein: 8g, Carbs: 52.3g, Fats: 14.1g

17. Rice Mushroom Salad with Herbs

Ingredients:

½ cup rice

1 cup button mushrooms

2 crushed garlic cloves

1 chopped onion

½ tsp dried basil

¼ tsp dried marjoram

1 tsp dried celery

1 tbsp olive oil

Salt and pepper to taste

Preparation:

Place rice at the bottom of a small pot and pour in 1 1/2 cups of water. Sprinkle with salt and bring it to a boil. Reduce the heat to medium-low and simmer until all the liquid has evaporated. Remove from the heat and set aside.

Preheat the oven to 375 degrees F. Grease a small baking pan with oil and rice. Set aside.

Heat up the olive oil in a small skillet. Add onions and garlic. Sprinkle with some salt and cook until translucent. Add mushrooms and continue to cook for 3-4 minutes, stirring constantly. Sprinkle with herbs, salt, and pepper.

Transfer to a baking dish and pour in about 1/4 cup of water or vegetable stock. Bake for 15 minutes.

When done, remove from the oven and let chill completely before serving.

Nutritional information per serving: Kcal: 526, Protein: 10g, Carbs: 88.6g, Fats: 15.3g

18. Eggplant Kale Salad and Pine Nuts

Ingredients:

1 small eggplant

1 cup chopped kale

1 tbsp pine nuts

¼ cup feta cheese

2 tbsp Parmesan cheese

2 tbsp Greek yogurt

1 tbsp olive oil

¼ tsp garlic powder

Salt to taste

Preparation:

Slice eggplant lengthwise and generously sprinkle with salt. Place in a large sieve and let it sit for 15 minutes.

Meanwhile, preheat the oven to 400 degrees F. Line a small baking dish with some parchment paper and set aside.

In a medium-sized bowl, combine together kale, pine nuts, feta cheese, parmesan, Greek yogurt, garlic powder, and salt. Mix all well and set aside. Rinse eggplant under cold running water and scoop out most of the flesh.

Brush each half with oil and fill with the kale mixture. Bake for 25 minutes.

When done, remove from the oven set aside to cool completely before serving.

Enjoy!

Nutritional information per serving: Kcal: 466, Protein: 18g, Carbs: 38g, Fats: 31g

19. Zucchini Garlic Salad

Ingredients:

1 large zucchini

2 garlic cloves

1 tbsp olive oil

1 tbsp balsamic vinegar

1/4 tsp salt

Preparation:

Rinse zucchini under cold running water and slice into about 1/2-inch round slices. Sprinkle with salt and let it sit for 10 minutes.

Meanwhile, preheat the grill to high. Rinse the zucchini and pat dry with some kitchen paper.

In a small bowl, whisk together olive oil, balsamic vinegar, salt, and garlic powder.

Brush zucchini with this mixture and grill for 3-4 minutes per side.

When done, let it chill completely before serving.

Enjoy!

Nutritional information per serving: Kcal: 163, Protein: 3.3g, Carbs: 8.4g, Fats: 13.8g

20. Mushroom Leek Salad with Rice

Ingredients:

½ cup brown rice

1 chopped leek

1 cup sliced mushrooms

1 chopped onion

1 chopped spring onion

1 chopped celery stalk

1 tbsp olive oil

2 tbsp soy sauce

1 tsp balsamic vinegar

¼ tsp dried basil

½ tsp salt

½ tsp red pepper flakes

Preparation:

Boil rice according to package instructions. Remove from the heat and set aside.

Heat up the oil in a wok pan and add chopped onions, spring onion, leek, and celery stalk. Sprinkle with some salt and cook for 4-5 minutes, stirring constantly.

Now, add mushrooms, soy sauce, and balsamic vinegar. Sprinkle with red pepper flakes, salt, basil, and optionally some pepper to taste. Continue to cook for 5 minutes, stirring occasionally.

Finally, add rice and give it a good stir.

Optionally, sprinkle all with finely chopped parsley and serve immediately.

Enjoy!

Nutritional information per serving: Kcal: 603, Protein: 14.2g, Carbs: 101g, Fats: 16.7g

21. Boiled Potato Salad with Mustard Seeds and Parsley

Ingredients:

1 large potato

1 sliced onion

1 crushed garlic clove

1 tbsp mustard seeds

1 tbsp finely chopped parsley

1 tbsp olive oil

2 tbsp lemon juice

Salt and pepper to taste

Preparation:

Peel potato and rinse well under cold running water. Cut into bite-sized pieces and place in a small pot. Pour in enough water to cover and bring it to a boil. Reduce the heat to medium and cook until fork tender. Remove from the heat and drain. Transfer to a bowl and cool for a while.

Meanwhile, peel and slice onion. Sprinkle with some salt and let it sit for 5 minutes. Rinse well and drain.

Transfer to a bowl along with garlic, mustard seeds, and parsley. Sprinkle with some salt and pepper to taste and drizzle with olive oil and lemon juice.

Serve cold.

Nutritional information per serving: Kcal: 361, Protein: 8.2g, Carbs: 45.8g, Fats: 18.6g

22.   Russian Vegetable Salad

Ingredients:

1 cup cooked beets

1 chopped tomato

1 chopped spring onion

1 tbsp salted capers

1 tbsp olive oil

1 tbsp lemon juice

Salt and pepper to taste

Preparation:

Trim and peel the beets. Cut into thin slices and place in a deep pot. Sprinkle with some salt and water enough to cover. Bring to a boil and cook for 10 minutes, or until soften. Remove from the heat and drain the water. Let it chill completely.

Wash the tomato and chop into bite-sized pieces. Place in a large bowl and set aside.

Chop the spring onions into small piceces and add it to the bowl with tomatoes.

In a small mixing bowl, combine capers, olive oil, lemon juice, salt, and pepper. Mix until well combined and set aside.

Finally, add beets to the bowl and drizzle all with the previously prepared dressing. Mix and serve immediately.

Enjoy!

Nutritional information per serving: Kcal: 264, Protein: 4.2g, Carbs: 21.4g, Fats: 15.1g

23.   Chickpea Sun Dried Tomato Salad

Ingredients:

1/3 cup roasted chickpeas

1 cup sun-dried tomatoes

¼ cup cooked quinoa

1 sliced cucumber

½ sliced red bell pepper

1 tbsp olive oil

1 tsp lemon juice

Salt and pepper to taste

Preparation:

Preheat the oven to 350 degrees. Line some parchment paper over a baking sheet and set aside.

Drain but don't rinse chickpeas. Sprinkle with some salt and transfer to baking sheet. Roast for 20-25 minutes or until golden brown. Remove from the oven and cool for a while.

Meanwhile, prepare the remaining ingredients. Place quinoa in a small pot and pour in 1/2 cup of water. Generously sprinkle with some salt and bring it to a boil.

Simmer for 10 minutes over medium heat, stirring occasionally. Remove from the heat and cool for a while.

Slice cucumber lengthwise and place in a bowl. Add the remaining ingredients and drizzle with olive oil and lemon juice.

Season with some salt and pepper to taste and serve immediately.

Nutritional information per serving: Kcal: 368, Protein: 10.1g, Carbs: 49.7g, Fats: 17.3g

24. Halloumi Cheese Salad

Ingredients:

3oz Halloumi cheese

1 orange

1 cup arugula

¼ cup pomegranate seeds

1 tbsp oil

1 tbsp orange juice

Salt

Preparation:

Grease a non-stick grill pan with oil and heat up over medium high heat. Slice the cheese into approximately 1/4-inch thick slices and grill for about 3 minutes on each side.

Sprinkle with salt and remove from the pan.

In a medium bowl, combine the remaining ingredients and add cheese. Sprinkle with orange juice and optionally some more salt.

Serve immediately.

Nutritional information per serving: Kcal: 553, Protein: 20.5g, Carbs: 32.4g, Fats: 39.4g

25. Grilled Peach Salad with Blue Cheese and Walnuts

Ingredients:

1 sliced peach

1 sliced purple onion

2 oz blue cheese

1 cup arugula

1oz walnuts

2 tbsp soy sauce

2 tsp rice vinegar

1 tsp orange zest

2 tsp black sesame seeds

¼ tsp ginger powder

Preparation:

Rinse the arugula thoroughly under running water using a large colander. Drain and torn into small pieces. Set aside.

Peel the onion and cut into thin slices. Set aside.

In a small bowl, whisk together soy sauce, rice vinegar, orange zest, sesame seeds, and ginger powder. Set aside.

Preheat a non-stick grill pan or an electric grill over high heat. Slice peach into 1/4-inch thich slices and brush with the soy sauce mixture. Grill for 3-4 minutes on one side. Carefully flip each piece and continue to grill for 2 more minutes.

Remove from the heat and place in a bowl. Add onions, blue cheese, arugula, and walnuts. Toss to combine and serve immediately.

Nutritional information per serving: Kcal: 543, Protein: 24.5g, Carbs: 33g, Fats: 37.2g

26. Moroccan Rice Salad

Ingredients:

¼ cup long grain rice

¼ cup drained lentils

1 cup sliced button mushrooms

2 chopped onions

¼ tsp cumin powder

¼ tsp cayenne pepper

¼ tsp smoked paprika

2 tbsp raisins

Preparation:

Preheat the oven to 350 degrees F.

Place rice in a small saucepan and pour in 1/2 cup of water. Sprinkle with some salt and bring it to a boil. Reduce the heat to medium-low and simmer until all the liquid has evaporated. Stir well and remove from the heat. Set aside.

Now, grease a small skillet with some oil and add onions. Sprinkle with cumin powder, cayenne pepper, and smoked paprika. Cook until translucent. Stir in mushrooms and continue to cook for 5 minutes, stirring occasionally. Stir in lentils and remove from the heat.

In a large bowl, combine together rice and the lentil mixture. Optionally, sprinkle with some more spices and place in a small baking pan. Add raisins and cook for 15-20 minutes.

When done, set aside to cool completely before serving.

Nutritional information per serving: Kcal: 495, Protein: 21.3g, Carbs: 103g, Fats: 1.2g

27. Vegetable Saute Salad

Ingredients:

1 chopped potato

½ chopped sweet potato

1 chopped red bell pepper

1 cup sliced cherry tomatoes,

1 chopped onion

1 garlic clove

2 tbsp flour

1 tsp cayenne pepper

1/2 tsp dried basil

1/2 tsp salt

1/2 cup vegetable stock

1/4 cup finely chopped parsley

1 tbsp olive oil

Preparation:

Heat the oil in a large non-stick frying pan. Add onions and garlic. Stir all well and cook until translucent.

Now, add potatoes and pour in vegetable stock. Season with salt, cayenne, and basil. Cook over medium heat until fork tender and then add sweet potato, red bell pepper, and cherry tomato. Stir in parsley and continue to cook until completely soft.

If necessary, add some more water or vegetable stock and stir in flour. Cook for 2-3 minutes and remove from the heat.

Cool completely before serving and enjoy!

Nutritional information per serving: Kcal: 487, Protein: 11.4g, Carbs: 82.3g, Fats: 15.2g

28. Black Bean Salad

Ingredients:

¼ cup rice

¼ cup black beans, soaked overnight

¼ small chopped red bell pepper

1 tsp olive oil

1 minced garlic clove

1 tbsp finely chopped cilantro

¼ tsp dried rosemary

¼ tsp smoked paprika

¼ tsp ground black pepper

1/8 tsp salt

Preparation:

Place the rice in a heavy-bottomed pot and cover with 3/4 cup of water. Bring it to a boil and then reduce the heat to low. Cook for 13-15 minutes.

Meanwhile, rinse and drain the beans. Place in a deep pot and cover with 1 cup of water. Bring it to a boil and cook for 20 minutes.

When done, drain well and set aside.

Preheat the oil in a large skillet over a medium-high heat. Add garlic and stir-fry for 2 minutes. Add beans, rice, and bell pepper. Sprinkle with rosemary, paprika, salt, and pepper. Stir well and cook for 3-4 minutes, stirring occasionally.

When done, remove from the heat and let it cool completely.

Serve cold.

Nutritional information per serving: Kcal: 421, Protein: 15g, Carbs: 78g, Fats: 6.2g

29. Mushroom Pepper Salad

Ingredients:

1 cup sliced button mushrooms

1 medium-sized chopped red bell pepper

¼ cup chopped broccoli

1 tbsp sesame seeds

1 tsp avocado oil

½ tsp rice vinegar

1 tsp soy sauce

¼ tsp chili powder

¼ tsp dried thyme

1/8 tsp ginger powder

1/8 tsp salt

Preparation:

Wash the pepper and cut lengthwise in half. Remove the seeds and cut into bite-sized pieces. Set aside.

Preheat the avocado oil in a large skillet over a medium-high heat. Add mushrooms and cook for 5 minutes, stirring occasionally.

Add chopped pepper and broccoli. Sprinkle with salt, thyme, and chili powder. Stir well and cook for 3-4 minutes.

Stir in the sesame seeds, soy sauce, vinegar, and ginger powder. Cook for 1 more minute and remove from the heat.

When chilled completely, add some more vinegar and serve.

Nutritional information per serving: Kcal: 127, Protein: 6.2g, Carbs: 15.9g, Fats: 6.3g

30. Tabbouleh Salad

Ingredients:

¼ cup bulgur

3 halved cherry tomatoes

¼ cup finely chopped cilantro

¼ cup sliced cucumber

1 tsp olive oil

2 tbsp finely chopped fresh mint

1 tsp lemon juice

1/8 tsp salt

1/8 tsp ground black pepper

Preparation:

Place bulgur in a deep bowl and pour in 1/2 cup of boiling water. Add olive oil and give it a good stir. Cover with a lid and let it stand for 20 minutes.

Now, combine all the remaining ingredients in a large salad bowl. Add bulgur and stir until well incorporated.

Optionally, add a pinch of red pepper or cayenne for spicier aroma.

Nutritional information per serving: Kcal: 231, Protein: 8.2g, Carbs: 41.6g, Fats: 5.7g

31. Zucchini Carrot Salad with Potatoes

Ingredients:

¼ cup sliced zucchini

1 medium-sized sliced carrot

1 large chopped potato

1 large sliced red bell pepper

¼ cup chopped eggplant

1 small chopped onion

1 finely chopped garlic clove

1 tsp olive oil

1 tsp soy sauce

1/8 tsp dried marjoram

1/8 tsp dried celery

1/8 tsp salt

1/8 tsp ground black pepper

Preparation:

First, wash and prepare the vegetables.

Peel the zucchini and carrot. Cut into thin slices and set aside.

Wash the bell pepper and cut lengthwise in half. Remove the seeds and stems. Cut into thin slices and set aside.

Combine eggplant, zucchini, potato, and carrot in a heavy bottomed pot. Add water enough to cover and sprinkle with some salt. Bring it to a boil and cook for 5 minutes. Remove from the heat and drain well.

In a small saucepan, heat up the olive oil over a medium-high heat. Add garlic and onions and stir-fry for 3-4 minutes. Add all the ingredients and cook for 5-7 minutes, stirring occasionally.

Remove from the heat and serve immediately.

Nutritional information per serving: Kcal: 433, Protein: 11g, Carbs: 90g, Fats: 6.3g

32. Apple Spinach Salad

Ingredients:

1 large Granny Smith's apple, cored and chopped

1 cup chopped spinach

1 cup chopped arugula

1 cup low fat cream

1 tsp apple cider vinegar

¼ tsp Italian seasoning

1 tbsp chopped walnuts

Salt and pepper

Preparation:

In a mixing bowl, combine low fat cream, apple cider vinegar, Italian seasoning, salt, and pepper. Mix until well combined and set aside.

Wash the apple and cut in half. Remove the core and cut into thin slices. Set aside.

In a large colander, combine spinach and arugula. Rinse under running water and drain. Set aside.

Now, combine apple, spinach, and arugula in a large salad bowl. Drizzle all with creamy dressing and give it a good stir.

Serve immediately.

Nutritional information per serving: Kcal: 461, Protein: 11.8g, Carbs: 57.8g, Fats: 21.6g

33. Mediterranean Fish Salad

Ingredients:

4 oz mackerel fillets

1 cup cherry tomatoes

¼ cup green olives, sliced

1 small sliced onion

1 tbsp lemon juice

½ tsp ground basil

¼ tsp ground garlic

¼ tsp ground rosemary

1 tbsp olive oil

Salt and pepper

Preparation:

Preheat the oven to 350 degrees. Line a piece of parchment paper over a baking sheet and set aside.

In a small mixing bowl, combine rosemary, olive oil, salt, and pepper. Mix until combined and set aside.

Rinse the fillets under running water and pat-dry with a

kitchen paper. Generously sprinkle with previously prepared mixture. Bake for 20 minutes, turning once halfway through. Remove from the oven and set aside to chill for a while.

Usinge a kitchen paper, soak up the excess oil and chop the fillets into bite-sized pieces.

Now, combine fish with the remaining ingredients on a serving plate and drizzle with the remaining olive oil mixture.

Give it a good stir and serve immediately.

Nutritional information per serving: Kcal: 486, Protein: 29.6g, Carbs: 14.5g, Fats: 35.1g

34. Tuna Kalamata Salad

Ingredients:

1 cup canned tuna

½ cup Kalamata olives, sliced

1 cup chopped Iceberg lettuce

1 small sliced red onion

1 chopped red bell pepper

1 tbsp olive oil

1 tbsp lemon juice

½ tsp Italian seasoning

Salt and red pepper

Preparation:

Using a large colander, rinse the lettuce under running water. Drain and torn with your hands into a small pieces. Place in a large salad bowl and set aside.

Remove the pits from olives and cut into thin slices.

Peel the onion and cut into thin slices.

Wash the bell pepper and cut lengthwise in half. Remove

the seeds and stem. Cut into small pieces and set aside.

In a small mixing bowl, combine olive oil, lemon juice, Italian seasoning, salt, and pepper. Mix until combined and set aside.

Now, combine lettuce, onion, and red bell pepper in a large salad bowl. Top with tuna and drizzle with previously prepared dressing.

Serve immediately.

Nutritional information per serving: Kcal: 306, Protein: 25.1g, Carbs: 11g, Fats: 18.4g

35. Green Bean Spinach Salad with Walnuts

Ingredients:

1 cup fresh baby spinach

1 cup green beans

1 garlic clove

2 tbsp chopped walnuts

1 tsp sunflower oil

Salt to taste

Preparation:

Rinse the green beans under running water. Drain and chop into bite-sized pieces. Transfer to a large pot and cover with water. Bring to a boil over medium-high heat. Cook for 10 minutes. Remove from the heat. Using a slotted spoon, drain and set aside to chill for a while.

Rinse the spinach using a colander. Drain well and torn into small pieces. Transfer to a large bowl and add green beans.

Drizzle with sunflower oil and minced garlic. Sprinkle with some salt and stir well.

Top with walnuts before serving.

Nutritional information per serving: Kcal: 183, Protein: 6.8g, Carbs: 11.5g, Fats: 14.1g

36. Quinoa Radish Salad

Ingredients:

½ cup quinoa

1 cup chopped radish

½ cup grated cabbage

½ cup feta cheese

1 tbsp finely chopped parsley

¼ tsp cayenne pepper

1 tsp balsamic vinegar

Olive oil

Salt to taste

Preparation:

In a heavy-bottomed pot, combine quinoa and 1 cup of water. Bring to a boil over medium-high heat. Reduce the heat to low and cook for 10-12 minutes, or until all the liquid has been evaporated. Remove from the heat and fluff with a fork. Set aside.

Trim off the outer leaves of radish. Rinse well under running water and transfer to a cutting board. Chop into thin strips and sprinkle with some vinegar.

In a large salad bowl, combine quinoa, radish, cabbage, and feta cheese. Sprinkle all with olive oil, salt, cayenne pepper, and parsley.

Give it a good stir and serve immediately.

Nutritional information per serving: Kcal: 271, Protein: 12g, Carbs: 32.1g, Fats: 10.7g

37. Sweet Potato Cheese Salad

Ingredients:

1 medium sweet potato

1 large onion

1 cup cottage cheese

1 tbsp olive oil

1 tbsp finely chopped parsley

Salt and pepper to taste

Preparation:

Peel the sweet potato and cut into small chunks. Place in a deep pot and add water enough to cover. Bring to a boil and cook for 10-15 minutes, or until fork-tender. Remove from the heat and drain well. Set aside to cool completely.

Peel the onion and cut into small pieces. Sprinkle with salt and let it stand for 10 minutes. Using a colander, rinse well and drain. Transfer to a large salad bowl along with sweet potato chunks and cottage cheese.

Sprinkle with olive oil, parsley, salt, and pepper. Mix until all well incorporated and serve immediately.

Enjoy!

Nutritional information per serving: Kcal: 488, Protein: 35.1g, Carbs: 46g, Fats: 18.7g

38.   Creamy Broccoli Pepper Salad

Ingredients:

1 cup chopped broccoli

1 cup Greek yogurt

1 small green pepper

½ tsp garlic powder

1 tbsp olive oil

1 tsp ground basil

Salt to taste

Preparation:

Using a large colander, rinse the broccoli under running water. Drain and chop into bite-sized pieces. Set aside.

Preheat the oil in a frying pan over a medium-high heat. Add broccoli and sprinkle with some salt. Cook for 10 minutes, or until soften. Remove from the heat and set aside to cool.

In a food processor, combine green pepper, Greek yogurt, garlic, basil, and salt. Pulse until smooth and creamy.

Drizzle the broccoli with yogurt mixture and give it a good

stir.

Refrigerate for 20 minutes before serving.

Nutritional information per serving: Kcal: 323, Protein: 23.7g, Carbs: 19g, Fats: 18.5g

39. Lentil Cucumber Salad

Ingredients:

1 cup canned lentils

1 small cucumber

¼ cup low fat cream

2 tbsp lemon juice

2 tbsp olive oil

1 tbsp finely chopped parsley

1 large tomato

1 small onion

1 minced garlic clove

½ tsp dried dill

Salt to taste

Preparation:

Wash the cucumber and cut into small chunks. Place in a food processor along with low fat cream, lemon juice, olive oil, garlic, dill, and salt. Pulse until smooth and creamy and set aside.

Wash the tomato and cut into bite-sized pieces. Set aside.

Peel the onion and cut into thin rings. Set aside.

In a large bowl, combine lentils, tomato, and onion. Pour over the creamy mixture and give it a good stir.

Refrigerate for 30 minutes before serving.

Enjoy!

Nutritional information per serving: Kcal: 323, Protein: 23.7g, Carbs: 19g, Fats: 18.5g

40. Creamy Egg Salad

Ingredients:

4 large eggs

1 cup cottage cheese

1 tbsp sour cream

1 large tomato

1 large purple onion

1 tbsp lemon juice

1 tbsp minced hazelnuts

Salt to taste

Preparation:

Place the eggs in a deep pot and add water enough to cover. Bring to a boil over medium-high heat. Cook for 10-12 minutes and remove from the heat. Using a slotted spoon, transfer to separate bowl with ice cold water. Let it cool for 2 minutes and then peel. Chop into small pieces and set aside.

Wash the tomato and cut into bite-sized pieces. Set aside.

Peel the lemon and cut into thin rings. Set aside.

In a mixing bowl, combine cottage cheese, sour cream, lemon juice, and salt. Optionally, add some herbs according to your taste. Mix until well combined and set aside.

Ina large bowl, combine eggs, tomatoes, and onion. Pour over the cheese mixture and give it a good stir. Mix until well combined and refrigerate for 20 minutes before serving.

Enjoy!

Nutritional information per serving: Kcal: 320, Protein: 30.3g, Carbs: 16.2g, Fats: 15.1g

41. Arugula Tomato Salad

Ingredients:

2 cups chopped arugula

2 medium-sized tomatoes

¼ cup crumbled feta cheese

1 tbsp lemon juice

1 minced garlic clove

½ tsp dried thyme

Salt and pepper to taste

Preparation:

Using a large colander, rinse the arugula under running water. Drain well and chop into small pieces. Set aside.

Rinse the tomatoes well and transfer to a cutting board. Cut into bite-sized pieces and set aside.

In a small mixing bowl, combine lemon juice, garlic clove thyme, olive oil, salt, and pepper. Mix until well combined and set aside.

In a large salad bowl, combine arugula, tomatoes, and feta cheese. Drizzle with previously prepared dressing and give it a good stir.

Refrigerate for 15 minutes before serving.

Nutritional information per serving: Kcal: 163, Protein: 9g, Carbs: 14.2g, Fats: 8.9g

42. Chicken Walnut Salad

Ingredients:

6 oz skinless and boneless chicken breast

1 cup baby spinach

1 small tomato, chopped

1 small onion, sliced

1 large cucumber, sliced

2 tbsp minced walnuts

1 tbsp olive oil

Salt to taste

Preparation:

Rinse the chicken under running water and pat-dry with a kitchen paper. Transfer to a cutting board and cut into bite-sized pieces. Set aside.

Preheat the oil in a large skillet over a medium-high heat. Add chicken and cook for 4-5 minutes, or until golden brown. Remove from the heat and set aside to cool completely.

Wash and prepare the remaining vegetables.

In a large salad bowl, combine spinach, tomatoes, onions, and cucumber. Drizzle with lemon juice and top with walnuts.

Serve immediately.

Nutritional information per serving: Kcal: 248, Protein: 23.8g, Carbs: 11.8g, Fats: 13.1 g

43. Tomato Greens Salad

Ingredients:

1 large chopped tomato

1 small sliced onion

1 cup Iceberg lettuce

1 cup chopped spinach

1 cup arugula

1 red bell pepper

1 tbsp avocado oil

1 tbsp apple cider vinegar

½ tsp sea salt

¼ tsp red pepper

Preparation:

In a large colander, combine lettuce, spinach, and arugula. Rinse well under running water and drain. Roughly chop with your hands and transfer to a large salad bowl. Set aside.

Wash the bell pepper and cut lengthwise in half. Remove

the seeds and chop into bite-sized pieces. Set aside.

In a small mixing bowl, combine avocado oil, apple cider vinegar, salt, and pepper. Mix until well combined and set aside.

Now, combine all vegetables in a salad bowl and drizzle with oil. Mix until well incorporated and serve immediately.

Nutritional information per serving: Kcal: 140, Protein: 5.4g, Carbs: 27g, Fats: 2.9g

44. Cheese Salad with Cucumber

Ingredients:

1 cup cottage cheese

2 large cucumbers, sliced

2 large eggs

1 cup Iceberg lettuce

1 tbsp almond oil

¼ tsp dried thyme

¼ tsp dried dill

½ tsp salt

¼ tsp smoked paprika

Preparation:

Wash the cucumbers and cut into small chunks. Sprinkle with some salt and set aside.

Place the eggs in a deep pot and cover with water. Bring to a boil over a medium-high heat. Cook for 10-12 minutes. Remove from the heat and transfer to a separate bowl with ice cold water. After few minutes, gently peel and cut into bite-sized pieces.

In a small mixing bowl, combine almond oil, dried thyme, dried dill, salt, and smoked paprika. Mix until combined and set aside.

Now, add eggs to a bowl with cucumbers and pour over the dressing. Give it a good stir and serve immediately.

Enjoy!

Nutritional information per serving: Kcal: 284, Protein: 24g, Carbs: 16.5g, Fats: 14.4g

45. Green Bean Radish Salad with Spicy Tuna

Ingredients:

½ cup canned green beans

1 large tomato

2 cups shredded radish

1 cup canned tuna

½ tsp chili powder

1 tbsp olive oil

¼ tsp dried thyme

¼ tsp ground cumin

Preparation:

Place the radish in a large colander and rinse well under running water. Drain and transfer to a cutting board. Shred or cut into thin strips and place in a large salad bowl. Set aside.

In a small mixing bowl, combine chili powder, olive oil, dried thyme, and ground cuming. Mix until combined and set aside.

Now, combine radish, chopped tomato, and green beans in

a bowl. Stir once and top with tuna.

Finally, drizzle all with spicy sauce and serve immediately.

Enjoy!

Nutritional information per serving: Kcal: 272, Protein: 25.8g, Carbs: 10g, Fats: 14.7g

46. Egg Onion Salad

Ingredients:

4 large eggs

2 medium-sized onions

1 grated carrot

1 cup spinach

1 tbsp lemon juice

1 tbsp olive oil

¼ tsp ground cumin

¼ tsp dried dill

Salt and pepper to taste

Preparation:

Peel the onions and cut into thin rings. Place in a small bowl and sprinkle with some salt. Let it sit for 10 minutes.

Place the eggs in a deep pot and cover with water. Bring to a boil over a medium-high heat. Cook for 10-12 minutes. When done, remove from the heat and transfer to a bowl with ice cold water. Let it chill for a while and then peel. Cut into bite-sized pieces and set aside.

In a small bowl, combine olive oil, lemon juice, ground cumin, dried dill, salt, and pepper. Mix until well combined and set aside.

Now, in a large salad bowl combine onions, eggs, spinach, and carrot. Drizzle with previously prepared dressing and give it a good stir.

Serve immediately.

Nutritional information per serving: Kcal: 266, Protein: 14.6g, Carbs: 14.9g, Fats: 17.2g

47. Cheese Lettuce Salad

Ingredients:

2 cups Iceberg lettuce

1 cup cottage cheese

2 tbsp canned corn

1 small chili pepper

1 tbsp lime juice

1 tbsp avocado oil

Salt to taste

Preparation:

Using a large colander, rinse the lettuce under running water. Drain and chop into small pieces. Set aside.

Cut the chili pepper in half and remove the seeds. Chop into small pieces and set aside.

In a large bowl, combine lettuce, cottage cheese, corn, and chili pepper. Drizzle with lime juice, avocado oil, and salt. Mix until well combined and serve immediately.

Nutritional information per serving: Kcal: 503, Protein: 41.8g, Carbs: 70.6g, Fats: 10g

48. Couscous Salad with Cucumber and Goat's Cheese

Ingredients:

¼ cup couscous

¼ cup soft goat's cheese

½ sliced cucumber

½ sliced purple onion

1 tbsp finely chopped parsley

1 tsp salt

¼ tsp ground white pepper

¼ tsp dried thyme

¼ tsp turmeric powder

1 tbsp freshly squeezed lemon juice

1 cup reduced-fat Greek yogurt

Preparation:

Place couscous in a small saucepan and pour in 1/3 cup of water. Sprinkle with some salt and optionally with some olive oil. Stir all well and bring to a boil. Reduce the heat to low and cover. Cook until all the liquid has evaporated, stirring occasionally. Remove from the heat and let it sit, covered, for another 10 minutes. Fluff couscous with a fork and set aside.

Heat a large wok pan over medium-high heat and optionally grease with some olive oil. Add onions and briefly cook, for 1-2 minutes.

Now, add couscous and sprinkle with parsley, salt, white pepper, thyme, and turmeric powder. Cook for 4-5 minutes, stirring constantly. Remove from the heat and transfer to a bowl. Add goat's cheese and cucumber. Drizzle with lemon juice and stir all well.

Serve with Greek yogurt.

Nutritional information per serving: Kcal: 459, Protein: 32.8g, Carbs: 53.2g, Fats: 12.9g

49. Asparagus Zucchini Salad

Ingredients:

10oz chopped asparagus

1 medium zucchini

¼ cup sliced radish

¼ cup soft goat's cheese

2 cups chopped baby spinach

2 tbsp drained green peas

1 tbsp pine nuts

1 tsp olive oil

1 tbsp lemon juice

½ tsp salt

Preparation:

Preheat the oven to 425 degrees F. Line a baking sheet with parchment paper and set aside.

Cut off dry ends of the asparagus and rinse well under cold running water. Place on the prepared baking sheet and sprinkle with salt. Optionally, drizzle with some olive oil and roast for 15-20 minutes. Remove from the oven and set aside.

Run zucchini through spiralizer and briefly cook in a wok pan over high heat.

In another bowl, combine the remaining ingredients and add asparagus. Sprinkle with salt, olive oil, and lemon juice.

Serve immediately.

Nutritional information per serving: Kcal: 440, Protein: 26.3g, Carbs: 25.9g, Fats: 24.3g

50. Quinoa Mozzarella Salad with Beans

Ingredients:

1 cup quinoa

2oz sliced mozzarella

½ cup drained green beans

1 chopped tomato

2 cup chopped spinach

1 tsp turmeric powder

½ tsp sea salt

¼ tsp chili powder

¼ tsp cumin powder

Preparation:

Place the quinoa in a heavy-bottomed pot. Add 2 cups of water and bring to a boil. Reduce the heat to low and cook for 12-15 minutes. When done, remove from the heat and set aside to cool. Fluff with a fork and set aside.

Using a large colander, rinse the spinach thoroughly under running water. Drain and chop into small pieces. Place in a large salad bowl, along with chopped tomato and green beans.

Sprinkle all with turmeric powder, sea salt, chili powder, and cumin powder. Add cheese and quinoa. Give it a good stir and serve immediately.

Enjoy!

Nutritional information per serving: Kcal: 437, Protein: 28.2g, Carbs: 52g, Fats: 14.3g

51. Kale Salad with Tomatoes and Corn

Ingredients:

2 cups chopped kale

¼ cup sliced radishes

½ cup drained corn

1 cup cherry tomatoes

½ cup cottage cheese

1 tbsp vegetable oil

1 tbsp lemon juice

¼ tsp salt

¼ tsp dried marjoram

Preparation:

Rinse kale thoroughly under cold running water and drain in a large colander. Set aside.

Rinse the cherry tomatoes and remove the stems. Cut each into halves and set aside.

Heat a small, non-stick grill pan over medium-high heat and briefly brown corn, for 5-6 minutes, stirring constantly.

Transfer to a bowl and add the remaining ingredients.

Sprinkle with oil, lemon juice, salt, and marjoram.

Serve immediately.

Nutritional information per serving: Kcal: 451, Protein: 26.2g, Carbs: 54.1g, Fats: 17.9g

52. Spicy Pepper Salad

Ingredients:

2 sliced red bell peppers

1 sliced carrot

1 diced chili pepper

½ chopped purple onion

¼ cup sliced Gouda

¼ cup grated sharp white cheddar

1 cup sliced cherry tomatoes

¼ chopped celery stalk

1 tbsp olive oil

1 tbsp lemon juice

2 slices whole grain bread

Preparation:

Wash the bell peppers and cut in half. Remove the seeds and stems. Chop into thin slices and set aside.

Peel the carrot and remove the top end. Cut into thin slices and set aside.

Wash the chili pepper and cut in half. Remove the seeds and finely dice. Set aside.

Rinse the cherry tomatoes and cut each in half. Set aside.

Roughly chop the bread slices into bite-sized pieces.

Now, combine bell peppers, carrot, chili pepper, onion, Gouda cheese, cheddar cheese, cherry tomatoes, celery stalk, and bread. Drizzle all with olive oil and lemon juice. Give it a good stir and serve immediately.

Enjoy!

Nutritional information per serving: Kcal: 441, Protein: 20.2g, Carbs: 53.8g, Fats: 17.2g

53. Waldorf Salad with Quinoa

Ingredients:

¼ cup uncooked quinoa

½ chopped apple

1 tbsp sultanas

1oz walnuts

¼ chopped celery stalk

2 tbsp freshly squeezed orange juice

1 tsp freshly squeezed lime juice

1 tsp brown sugar

¼ tsp cinnamon powder

1/8 tsp ground nutmeg

Preparation:

Place the quinoa in a deep pot and add ½ cup of water. Bring to a boil over medium-high heat. Reduce the heat to low and simmer for 10 minutes. Remove from the heat and let it cool completely.

Wash the apple and cut in half. Remove the core and chop

one half into bite-sized pieces. Reserve the rest in the refrigerator.

Now, combine quinoa, apple, sultanas, walnuts, and celery in a large salad bowl. Drizzle with orange juice, lime juice, brown sugar, cinnamon powder, and ground nutmeg. Mix until well combined

Serve immediately.

Nutritional information per serving: Kcal: 438, Protein: 19.4g, Carbs: 54.2g, Fats: 13.2g

ADDITIONAL TITLES FROM THIS AUTHOR

70 Effective Meal Recipes to Prevent and Solve Being Overweight: Burn Fat Fast by Using Proper Dieting and Smart Nutrition

By

Joe Correa CSN

48 Acne Solving Meal Recipes: The Fast and Natural Path to Fixing Your Acne Problems in Less Than 10 Days!

By

Joe Correa CSN

41 Alzheimer's Preventing Meal Recipes: Reduce or Eliminate Your Alzheimer's Condition in 30 Days or Less!

By

Joe Correa CSN

70 Effective Breast Cancer Meal Recipes: Prevent and Fight Breast Cancer with Smart Nutrition and Powerful Foods

By

Joe Correa CSN

www.ingramcontent.com/pod-product-compliance
Lightning Source LLC
Chambersburg PA
CBHW052023070526
44584CB00016B/1870